What Others Are Saying about
The Transformation Challenge

"This is much more than a book . . . it's a proven framework and blueprint for success in both business and life! I have implemented the Becoming Your Best Leadership Model into my organization and witnessed firsthand the dramatic effects it had on our team and thus our company! In my opinion, the Six Step Process is the "secret sauce" of it all! My advice—commit to it, execute on it, and watch the transformation take place!"

—John W. Fitzpatrick, President/CEO, Force Marketing

"*The Transformation Challenge—A New Approach to Winning in Business and Life,* is a must-read book for executives and managers trying to get the best from themselves and those around them. This is a poignant and powerful collection of insights from one of the great business and people leaders on what it takes to become a better leader, manager, employee, parent, and friend."

—David Williams, Founder, CEO, Board Member,
Leadership Coach, Forbes/HBR Contributor,
Book Author, Entrepreneur

"In our current, diverse world with so many challenges and problems, this book is a must read. The Six-Step Process has been such a life-changing solution for me in my personal and professional life. It is a tool that makes all the difference. If you want to know why you haven't realized your vision, this book will show you the current reality and the root cause. The Transformational Challenge is a process worth the effort. I highly recommend this book!"

—Julie Richardson, President/CEO Energy Efficiency Inc.

"The Shallenbergers have done it again! *The Transformation Challenge* provides a template to strategically map out how to overcome any challenge. There are very few playbooks that can be applied in every facet of life, and *The Transformation Challenge* is one to top them all."

—**Dean Griess**, Executive Learning Leader, Charles Schwab

"We've been working with Rob and using the Becoming Your Best system for two years now, and the results have been amazing. We had been looking for a sales improvement and motivational program for A Place for Mom's 500-person, work-from-home sales force. The BYB program, with its powerful emphasis on skill set and mind-set, was exactly what we were looking for. Our advisers are motivated, excited, engaged, and performance is up! BYB is not just a good idea, it's a system for all aspects of your life that is driving positive results for A Place for Mom, our employees, and our customers."

—**Sean D. Kell**, CEO, A Place for Mom, Inc.

"The Six-Step Process outlined in *The Transformation Challenge* book has had a significant positive impact on my business, it has helped me through many tough multi-million dollar obstacles. Rob and Steve have a way to enlighten you and help you turn hard business problems into win-win solutions. I have shared this book with many partners and friends. It is fantastic!"

—**Cory Moore**, Executive Vice President, Big-D Construction

"The process laid out in this book will make you a better executive. It makes you a better thinker and will create better results. This is a high-impact process."

—**Mark W. Brugger**, President & CEO,
DiamondRock Hospitality Company, NYSE: DRH

"Coming from the success of *Becoming Your Best,* with its eye-opening concepts and strategies that embody the true essence of a leader, *The Transformation Challenge* is another revolutionary movement that will help anyone tap into the best version of themselves. The Six-Step Process is a doable approach to make positive changes in an organization and in a person's career or personal life. Obstacles are inevitable and opportunities are everywhere, so the clear, realistic guide that Steve and Rob have developed in overcoming difficulties and achieving success sheds light in the uncertainties of change and growth. As explained in this life manual, everyone is a leader (of your own life or of an organization), and *The Transformation Challenge* is an essential read in order to become an inspiring, effective one . . . and consistently keeps you on your toes. Being at your best is the true essence of a great leader."

—Jean Henri D. Lhuillier, President and CEO,
P. J. Lhuillier Group of Companies

"This book is spot on. *The Transformation Challenge* is a clear and simple road map to personal and business success. The Six Steps will lead you to find new thoughts, approaches, and best outcomes. The "who, what, when" template is applicable to any type of situation you want to improve."

—Rona Rahlf, President, Utah Valley Chamber

"Rob and Steve's new book, *The Transformation Challenge*, is a call to action that hits eerily close to home. They take us through the "Six-Step Process" with real world stories that any one of us could be the leading actor in. From personal life to business, their heartfelt stories and practical tools position us for success in our life's goals and ambitions. Rob and Steve challenge us to find our vision for the future and provide actionable tools that we can implement immediately with our teams and families. As they said, "It's time to live a life by design, not by default." I will be implementing the *Six-Step Process*!"

—Justin Erickson, Husband, Father, and CEO/Owner,
Harbor Wholesale Foods

"Under the tutelage of Steve and Rob Shallenberger and by following the steps outlined in *The Transformation Challenge: A New Approach to Winning in Business and Life,* your life and business will be transformed, no doubt. Simply put, you'll achieve more out of life and more quickly. I've been the beneficiary of the wisdom taught by these two outstanding gentlemen for decades, and their insights have helped me build two large global companies. They walk the walk, not just talk the talk. I cannot recommend this book more highly."

—**Dallin A. Larsen**, Founder and CEO, Vasayo

"Imagine finding a book that is the missing link in your personal and professional improvement. I found that here in Steve and Rob's latest book. This book has transformed my approach to problem-solving by using my vision and goals as the starting point. I will be forever grateful that I had the chance to read this book and apply it to my life and business. The real-life experiences shared and the approach to the principles taught are spot on. A must read for professional and personal growth and positive change."

—**Rick Taylor**, Owner, Taylor Fire Protection Services

"Rob and Steve nailed it! I loved this book from start to finish. I am going to apply their model in my own life."

—**Randy Garn**, *New York Times* Best-Selling Author

"If you are looking to excel both personally and within your organization, this book is a must read!"

—**David Gordon**, Managing Partner, Monumental Markets

"Most people believe they know how to solve problems, but few people actually use a defined method or disciplined approach to problem-solving. In *The Transformation Challenge,* Rob and Steve Shallenberger give you both. The Six-Step Process applies to any aspect of your life that you are looking to improve. This book does more than transform your approach to problem-solving, it transforms your results!"

—**Gary Marlowe**, Fighter Pilot

"After learning about Becoming Your Best, I had to have more! Their approach has helped me become a better person, a better leader, and a better friend. I know this book will help you take that next step!"

—**Kenneth M Hanifan**, President, Slater Hanifan Group

"*Challenge accepted!* The Becoming Your Best team presents a practical tool to create lasting change in any facet of your life. The power of the Six-Step Process is in its simplicity; a formula that you can carry with you the rest of your life. Thank you to Rob and Steve for unlocking the keys to creating a meaningful transformation!"

—**Steve Mena**, VP of Operations, Premier Healthcare Services

"Everyone needs to read and absorb the strategies in this brilliant book by my friends Rob and Steve Shallenberger. The strategies will change your life! I've known Rob and Steve for a number of years and I can tell you that they come from the heart and truly care about making a positive difference in the lives of others!"

—**James Malinchak**, Featured on ABCs Hit TV Show *Secret Millionaire*,
Author of *Millionaire Success Secrets*,
Founder of www. MillionaireFreeBook. com

"*The Transformation Challenge* encourages us to approach all of life's challenges like a seasoned CEO! Steve and Rob Shallenberger present a simple yet ***solid, repeatable process*** to approach business and everyday problems in a way that produces ***positive, predictable results***. I would highly recommend this book as reference for anyone who has sporadic or routine issues that affect their long-term goals. Our team has personally followed this unique system and has experienced unprecedented improvement in our company culture, as well as our bottom line!"

—**David E. Wayt**, President, My Logistics Partner, Inc.

"Our companies have been actively engaged with Steven Shallenberger for over 30 years. We have seen a transformational change in our associates and stakeholders throughout our companies while implementing these principles and processes from this book!"

—**David Clark**, President, Energy Services

"I am too busy. Maybe you are as well. It impacts my family, my health and my overall well being. As I examined my current reality, I realized I needed to reframe my issue. I am applying the Transformation Challenge to my issue. In a short period of time I have framed my issue, set my smart goals, and for the first time I see my new path clearly before me. This is an amazing process! I highly recommend it to you if you are seeking meaningful change in your life."

—**Mark Holland**, President, Intermountain STAFFING and Ascend HR

"*The Transformation Challenge—A New Approach to Winning in Business and Life* is a benchmark for authentic leadership. The concepts in this innovative exploration for winning in our personal lives and in garnering high-level success in any business organization is clear and powerful as it unveils the hidden key to productivity and creativity. Certainly, the contents of this book will have a greater impact on people in the workplace and the varied phases of life far beyond any current recollection—a remarkable read!"

—**David Glen Hatch**, D.M.A.
International Concert Pianist/Recording Artist,
Arranger, Master Teacher, Adjudicator, Clinician, Author

The
TRANSFORMATION
CHALLENGE

A new approach to winning in business and life!

STEVEN & ROBERT SHALLENBERGER

First Edition

ISBN 978-0-07-183998-4

For information regarding special discounts for bulk purchases, please contact Becoming Your Best Global Leadership at (888) 690-8764.

FROM STEVE:

This book is dedicated to you who desire to reach new heights and make your Good Better, and your Better Best! Because of YOU, the world will be a better place. Thank you for your example and tireless efforts.

FROM ROB:

To my extraordinary wife, Tonya, and our four amazing children, whose generation will shape our future. Also, to my parents, who are a light to the world.

Acknowledgments

I (Steve) am forever indebted to the remarkable mentors and advisers who have deeply touched my life: Cal Clark, David Conger, Stephen R. Covey, Robert K. Dellenbach, William N. Jones, Thomas S. Monson, Gardner H. Russell, Lael J. Woodbury, and all of those who have had a powerful influence for good. May I pass it along!

David C. Clark, my amazing business partner of almost four decades, who has been ever encouraging and supportive. To my extraordinary friends at Synergy Companies. YOU are among the best! I appreciate the years of experience with my friends at Eagle Systems International and Covey Leadership. You continue to change the world for good.

To my Harvard CAN Group, the Young President's Organization and forum members.

To my friends and associates at the Utility companies, and in the Energy Services Industry, who continue to work on world-class services.

We are grateful for our family and extended family members (Humpherys, Quarles, and Shallenbergers), including our ancestors, grandparents, and parents. Thanks, Mom and Dad!

To Rob, Dave, Steven, Tom, Daniel, Anne, and their spouses and the grandchildren! To each of our children, and Roxanne—you have had such a huge impact on my life.

We appreciate the scores of individuals who have provided encouragement and the many who reviewed the manuscript and offered valuable recommendations, including but not limited to Jim Amos, Gary Marlowe, Chad Erickson, Jon Meacham, Kimball Anderson, Carl Bacon, Lothaire Bluth, Matt Clark,

Stephen M. R. Covey, Casey Davis, Jim Evans, Joseph Grenny, Winn Egan, Wynn Hemmert, Erick Henry, Jerry Johnson, Pete Landre, Dallin Larsen, Jean Henri Lhuillier, Bruce Matulich, Crystal Maggelet, David McDougal, Jenni Miller, Jean Philbert Nsengimana, Suzanne Oliver, Alan Osmond, Marshall Paepke, David Price, Doug Price, Dane and Barbara Quittner, Julie Richardson, Emery Rubagenga, Jamie Thorup (Mr. Amazing), Sal Vaccaro, Paul Warner, David Wayt, Ron Williams, David Olsen, and Jennifer Tanner. And also Angela Eschler, Michele Preisendorf, Kimberly Kay, and Chris Yates of EschlerEditing.com.

Steven and Rob Shallenberger

Contents

Foreword

I have spent my career studying what we call "vital behaviors"—small actions that yield outstanding results. For example, we've found that small changes in the way you communicate can heal a relationship. We've identified small adjustments in the design of your environment that produce huge changes in health and fitness. And we've found simple tactics that can help create rapid, profound, and sustainable changes in organizational performance.

The process the Shallenbergers describe in *The Transformation Challenge* is as vital as they come. *The Transformation Challenge* will help you and your team develop both the mind-set and skill set to solve any problem, identify a clear path forward, and transform your dreams into reality.

Early in our research on *Crucial Conversations*, we did a field experiment that produced a surprising result. We found people standing in long lines and sent confederates to cut in line in front of them. Few spoke up. Unless . . . just prior to a line jumper cutting in front of them, *they heard a skillful person address the exact same problem.* In one condition of the experiment we staged a line cutting between confederates just prior to sending someone to jump the line in front of a real subject. In this condition, not only did the real subject speak up far more often, they tended to use *the exact same words* they heard our skilled confederate use a minute earlier!

In moments of emotional turmoil, few of us know *what* to do. We don't like what's happening, but we can't think clearly to get ourselves out of our current mess. In this insightful and practical book, Steve and Rob Shallenberger join you in line in any place in life where you currently are. They help you reexamine frustrations at work, at home, or in your personal life. They stand beside you in your confusion and point the way up and out.

Not only are Steve and Rob qualified by study and research, but their remarkable life stories make them trustworthy guides to help you transform your work and life.

The Transformation Challenge is a challenge to take any issue, either personal or professional, and apply Steve and Rob's Six-Step Process to develop a way forward that will guide you to winning results *every time.*

This potent process can be used to address any weighty issue that you might face such as how to increase sales, decrease turnover, improve the customer experience, save a relationship, end an addiction, improve your health or become financially self-reliant.

This is a book that will give you hope, encouragement, and inspiration.

The Transformation Challenge should be a required text for anyone and any organization. I am confident it will be one of the best investments you ever make!

—Joseph Grenny, #1 *New York Times* Best-Selling Author of *Crucial Conversations* & *Influencer*

Introduction

Think about the biggest issues (problems or opportunities) you are dealing with right now, either in your business or personal life. Maybe you're trying to hit a sales goal, or your team has too much turnover, or you would like to help a struggling department soar. Maybe your health isn't where you want it, or your relationships could be better.

Whatever the issue, imagine if you had a reliable process that empowered you to navigate change and solve *any* of your challenges, problems, or opportunities. What if that process provided an actionable plan and pathway that would turn your dreams and opportunities into a reality? What would that process be worth to you personally, professionally, and in your relationships? To be sure, it would be a skill so transformative its full value couldn't adequately be measured. Imagine how great you will feel and the energy it will bring to your team when you not only successfully navigate change and solve your problems, but you exceed your expectations.

This is the heart of the Transformation Challenge: to apply our proprietary Six-Step Process to any issue in your life—from the business-oriented to the personal—and discover how the process transforms the issue into a positive outcome. It may seem like a tall order, but the Six-Step Process provides you with an incredibly simple and powerful mechanism that illuminates and transforms challenges, issues, goals, and opportunities into brilliant plans that lead to greater peace, happiness, and success.

Before we embark on this journey together, you may be wondering about the genesis of the Transformation Challenge and the

Six-Step Process. They are rooted in the professional and personal experiences of a father-and-son team.

Together, we've had the good fortune to be involved in a worldwide movement called *Becoming Your Best*, where we have trained organizations of all sizes around the world, including the Dallas Cowboys, PepsiCo, Charles Schwab, Make-a-Wish, and many others.

And it all began nearly forty years ago when Steve, at age twenty-six, bought his first company.

It started with three hundred employees and quickly grew to more than one thousand. Thus began a journey that saw Steve start or buy eleven different companies in four different industries. Over several decades, he reached the peaks of success and endured major setbacks and failures. If your journey in the world of business or through life has had ups and downs, you can probably relate to some of the challenges Steve faced.

It was at age thirty-two, with a family of five children, that Steve suffered what he considered his biggest setback. A confluence of business-related events left Steve on the hook for millions of dollars. Things looked bleak. He didn't have the means to pay the money, nor did he have any obvious way forward that seemed even remotely hopeful. From every angle, it appeared that all was lost. This was truly a discouraging time.

But in the calculus of hope, one cannot quantify the power of the human spirit.

Over the course of seven long years, Steve scraped, saved, and worked tirelessly, often spending sixteen-plus hours a day in the office to pay off more than $10 million in business debt and obligations. Initially, the situation felt dire. There were times when he didn't know if he would even be able to make payroll and take care of his employees. He would often wake up at 2:00 a.m. wondering how he was going to survive. It may have been easier to simply walk away from the business and leave creditors hanging. Instead, he developed a plan, went to work, and ultimately satisfied every debt.

Through that refining process, he learned critical life and business lessons that fueled his success in multiple future ventures.

He decided that he'd never again owe another person a single penny, and that's how his future companies went on to make millions—by applying the lessons he learned during those difficult, lean years. It is interesting to note that during that busy time, he not only satisfied the $10 million debt, but he also maintained a solid relationship with his wife and successfully raised their six children. He's now been married for more than 45 years!

During that transformative period, Steve learned from great mentors, such as Zig Ziglar, Earl Nightingale, Dennis Waitley and many others. He developed a close personal friendship with Stephen R. Covey, his college professor, who served on Steve's board for seventeen years, while Steve, in turn, served on Stephen's board at the Covey Leadership Center for five years.

Throughout his journey of leading thousands of employees, Steve had an epiphany. He realized that no matter the person and no matter their situation, many encounter similar challenges and have similar concerns, both on a professional and personal level. One of the greatest difficulties people have is finding a way to navigate change, address their problems, and transform challenges into opportunities. The Six-Step Process evolved from this epiphany.

While Steve's personal experience was based on helping teams, leaders, and businesses on the ground, his oldest son Rob took to the skies.

Rob spent eleven years in the U. S. Air Force as an officer, F-16 fighter pilot, and Air Force One Advance Agent. He flew more than 750 flights in the fighter jet.

In the Air Force, Rob quickly learned the importance of having a solid plan to execute the mission. As you can imagine, fighter pilots facing life-or-death stakes cannot afford to have haphazard plans or a willy-nilly approach to problem solving. Rather, they work in a culture of meticulous planning, execution, and attention to detail. Even with the most detailed plans, a fighter pilot must additionally think about contingencies and what happens when the plan doesn't go exactly as planned—as happens to all of us in life.

Full immersion in these types of planning processes shaped Rob's approach toward his own life. Rob has been married for nineteen years and has four beautiful children. He has used this same fighter-pilot approach to help his marriage as well as to help his children accomplish things that at first seemed difficult or even impossible to them.

After he finished an MBA in his thirties and transitioned to civilian life, he realized that his experiences in the cockpit could provide any organization a useful perspective on how to navigate change and problem solve. Rob also found that this fighter pilot approach could help others build stronger personal relationships, navigate change in their personal life, and help people achieve their individual dreams. It's an approach that promotes meticulous planning, discipline in execution, and creativity in problem solving.

Just as Steve had discovered with teams and organizations, Rob found that people are craving something that will help them find more hope, happiness, and peace in their personal lives. Almost everyone is dealing with a challenge of some sort, they just need to know how to face it.

When we started a leadership and training company called Becoming Your Best Global Leadership, it was obvious to both of us that our clients needed: a simple, effective, and customizable process to navigate change and solve problems at any level of their organization.

With Steve's leadership experience in business along with Rob's training in planning and execution, we realized that we had the ingredients to create a powerful process—one that could really help people and their organizations.

That's where the Transformation Challenge comes in.

Over the years, people just like you, along with many organizations, have taken the Transformation Challenge and used the Six-Step Process (which will be explained in chapter 1) to achieve results that previously seemed daunting, and perhaps impossible. These people and organizations are now armed with a process that has saved them countless amounts of time, money, and energy. It is a process deeply embedded in their cultures.

The real question is why does this matter to you? Well, have you ever felt like you or your team were treading water? Just stuck in one place, expending time and energy, yet going nowhere? We've all felt like that at different points in our lives.

As you read, you will discover why many people and teams spend countless amounts of time and energy on problems, but never seem to make real progress toward fulfilling their vision or goals. It simply doesn't have to be that way any longer.

When you take the Transformation Challenge, you will discover how and why the Six-Step Process is so effective. The Six Steps aren't just a process for you or your team to learn; it's a new, fresh way of thinking! When you use the Six-Step Process you will possess a powerful way to transform your challenges into opportunities for the rest of your life. The Six Steps will shift the culture in your organization, give teams the tools and processes to find solutions and navigate any type of change. It's a breath of fresh air for teams to have a process to use as a template rather than just being left to their own devices to wing it.

The Transformation Challenge is built upon correct and wise principles of success that will provide you with hope, encouragement, action, and a positive way forward. In short, this book and process will help you solve problems, achieve goals, and improve how things work in your life, relationships, and organizations. It will help you make a difference for good wherever you go.

For a *free* Six-Step Process Quick Start Guide, visit www.TheTransformationChallenge.com. You can use this free template as you go through this book.

We wish you all the best in this exciting journey as you take the Transformation Challenge and apply the Six-Step Process.

CHAPTER 1

The Transformation Challenge— Six-Step Process

Imagine you're a manager on a high-stakes project. An employee comes to you with a concerned look and says, "We just got a call from our buyer. He says if we don't adjust the quantities and start delivering on time, he's going to pull the contract and find another supplier."

Now imagine that you're a member of a team working on a project that's on target to hit a major deadline. That is, until half the team is lured to another company by a headhunter, leaving you short on staff during the final, critical stretch of the project.

Now let's take a step away from business and consider your personal life. What if your doctor tells you that you need to radically alter your diet and fitness or you may face serious health problems? Or, what if you have a strained relationship with a friend, spouse, or child and you're not sure where to go from here? How do you respond to these types of situations?

Every day, all over the world, people and organizations face thousands of similar situations. After reading those brief examples, you might be wondering how this book applies to you.

Certainly, you have things you would like to transform in your life right now. It could be solving a complex business problem, finding a way to increase sales, or trying to become a better leader. Maybe you feel paralyzed because you feel as if you're constantly putting out proverbial fires instead of tapping into the power of your abilities and the abilities of those around you.

If you're not in the business world, you may be reading this book because a friend shared it with you or you may want to make changes in your life that go beyond business. Maybe it could be because you want to foster a better relationship with someone close to you, have better health, achieve a financial goal, or increase your own sense of self-worth.

The possibilities for why you are reading this book are infinite. Whatever the reason, the draw to this book likely stems from a desire to succeed. So, congratulations for opening the book and starting the journey.

Whether you hold a title of manager or not is irrelevant. Everyone is a leader in some capacity, because at a minimum you are leading your own life. Think about this, you will lead a life by design or you will live a life by default.

Whether leading a team or their own life, *great leaders first focus on what they want to create (the vision) and then figure out the real issue standing between their current reality and vision.* In other words, they get to the root causes of the obstacles that stand between their current reality and their desired outcome or vision. Once they understand that, they can identify the best options, develop a concrete plan, and evaluate the results. The way a leader approaches a problem or opportunity with his or her team will make the difference between their success or failure.

You would think knowing how to navigate change and problem-solving is intuitive and that most managers know how to do this; however, you might be surprised to see what we found. During the past four years we have researched how organizations and individuals navigate change and problem solve. Though it doesn't really matter the size of the organization, in our research we decided to evaluate 50 organizations with 100+ employees and more than $15 million in annual revenue. In each organization, we would ask managers how they approached a problem or opportunity both personally and with their team, and what steps they would use to develop a plan to address it.

Interestingly not a single organization had a common approach to navigate change or problem-solve. Almost every manager had a different response to how they addressed the problem. Even within the same organization, managers had a totally different approach. In fact, 88 percent of managers didn't have a specific process or framework to approach a problem or opportunity, let alone lead their team through a problem-solving process.

Think about what that means!

Within every one of those organizations, each manager and department is effectively speaking a different language. Just like at the Tower of Babel, teams within organizations speak a multitude of languages—but do not communicate. The medical profession calls this the Tower of Babel Syndrome. It refers to a lack of standardization in medical terminology that can result in miscommunication and significant errors. The same concept applies to navigating change in an organization.

So, if one manager is trying to address a problem with their non-aggressive, personalized approach, and another manager is using a more clashing approach, it's almost like they are trying to communicate in a foreign language—it rarely yields great results. This disparity in how employees and managers approach problems has led to millions in lost revenue, countless communication challenges, and significant misalignment and employee frustration—not to mention the wasted time and energy.

What most of these managers were unintentionally saying is that every time they needed to address a problem or new opportunity, they were winging it. Which, not surprisingly, resulted in "winging it" results. In most cases, it's not their fault because they haven't been shown or taught a better way.

Fortunately, the Transformation Challenge and Six-Step Process will help solve this challenge and can literally transform the way an organization plans and executes, dramatically improving results across the board. The Six Steps establish a common language, process, and thought-pattern for those in the organization to address any issue and navigate crucial change.

From the leaders' perspective, the Six-Step Process is a way of thinking about your problems or opportunities to help you establish a clear path forward. It is an angle of entry that gives you the confidence, peace, and calm to achieve results that previously may have seemed difficult or even impossible.

By developing this skill set, you will make a positive impact with every decision you encounter, no matter how big or how small. What's more, you'll become more effective in everything you do, at every level. You'll contribute more to those around you in both your personal and professional life.

At this point, you're probably asking, what *is* the Transformation Challenge and the Six-Step Process?

The Transformation Challenge, if you choose to accept it, is for you to choose a specific challenge in your organization or personal life and use our proprietary Six-Step Process to develop a plan and way forward to solve it.

That's it.

The beauty is when you finish this book, you'll have not only a plan for solving your most pressing challenge or opportunity, you will also have a process you can continue to rely on to navigate change for the rest of your life.

This will change the way you address problems in the workplace. There are now many organizations around the world that live by the Six-Step Process. Anytime they face a new problem or opportunity, they automatically go to the Six Steps, which has saved them countless money, time, and energy.

Whether it is transforming something in your business world or your personal world, we promise that when you take the Transformation Challenge and use our proprietary Six-Step

Process, it will help you blaze a path forward, bringing hope, excitement, and transformation. Not only that, when you take the Transformation Challenge for yourself, succeed, and then challenge someone else to do the same, you unleash a force for positive change that has the potential to become exponential. A domino-effect of transformations.

We wanted you to experience the Six Steps through the lens of others so that you can clearly see and feel how it relates to you. The stories in this book are from real people who were facing complex circumstances. In their stories, you will see the Transformation Challenge in action, and how the Six-Step Process helped them accomplish what had previously seemed impossible to many of them.

As with the people whose stories you read, if you want to see real progress in your life or with your team, you must act. To experience those transformations—and to get those results— you must do more than read the pages. Transformation requires action. After all, if you continue doing the same old thing, you will get the same old results.

Learning is all well and good, but the real power of the Transformation Challenge comes through *applying* the Six-Step Process.

That is why we're extending a personal, two-part invitation:

First, take the Transformation Challenge yourself as you read each chapter.

Second, after you have taken the challenge yourself, share the Transformation Challenge with someone else.

When you take the Transformation Challenge and apply the Six-Step Process in your life, you will quickly see how it revolutionizes the way you approach any problem or opportunity. This process will allow you to take any issue and think about it in a powerful, methodical way rather than doing what most people tend to do: procrastinate action or avoid action altogether. Those who do act typically go directly from problem to solution— which may never address the real issue causing the problem in the first place. Which means a temporary fix may get you somewhat acceptable results, but perhaps not the scale or scope of change you had hoped to see.

Before we get into the Six Steps, let's look at this from one more angle that will most likely impact you. How many great ideas have you had floating around in your brain that never left the "good intentions" phase?

Consider Lydie. We met Lydie two years ago in Rwanda when we were doing a Leadership Conference for two hundred entrepreneurs. She had always wanted to build a school to help the impoverished children of Rwanda, who in many cases, weren't getting the education they needed to break the poverty cycle. She had been gnawing on this idea for more than a decade, but it never moved beyond the "good intention" phase.

During that conference, every participant took the Transformation Challenge. Each participant had only one hour to go through the Six-Step Process. Lydie decided to use her hour to come up with ways to make her dream of building a school a reality. Lydie, with just a little coaching, developed a great plan. But did the Six-Step Process work? Was it the catalyst that launched her idea into action mode?

Two years later, we were back in Rwanda for a follow-up conference and we ran into Lydie. She excitedly told us that not only had she accomplished her dream to build a school, she had just finished building her *second* school. She'd literally blessed the lives of thousands of people—the students, their families, and their communities—because of her work.

As it has countless times, the Transformation Challenge showed how it got its name: the process transformed Lydie's dream into a thriving reality. It took years of good intentions and transformed them into an actionable plan. Her previously dormant idea was now a thriving reality in less than two years. In her words, she said, "I hadn't done anything in ten years and probably never would, had I not taken the Transformation Challenge and used the Six-Step Process!" To her credit, once she had the plan, she acted on it.

Since this is a book about you and/or your team, take a moment and come up with a brief list of things you would really like to improve in your life or in your organization. Write them below, on a notepad, or on your device—somewhere you won't lose it:

1.

2.

3.

4.

5.

6.

7.

We'll ask you to keep this list, either here in the book or on one of your devices, so that it can be on the forefront of your mind as you go through each of the Six Steps.

Now look over your list and think about each item. How would most people approach those problems or opportunities?

Based on our experience and research, most people will either (1) avoid confronting the problem in hopes that they just magically improve, or (2) they set a New Year's Resolution or similar turn-over-a-new-leaf goal, which generally fizzles out after a couple of weeks. That tends to be human nature.

It's interesting to see how this phenomenon manifests itself in a team setting.

While researching organizations, we found that the way most people and teams attempt to solve problems or develop a plan is exactly backward (in our opinion). Most people and teams start primarily focused on the problem. They throw money, time, or effort *at* the problem and end up with mixed results—at best. Sometimes they get lucky, but most of the time, they end up in a similar, or worse, position.

In a chaotic system like that—essentially no system at all—the odds of success are akin to that of blindly throwing darts at a dartboard.

For example, on an individual level, imagine someone who you've known in the past who tried to overcome an addiction, whatever the kind. Where was most of their time and energy likely focused? Usually, on the problem—in this case, on the addiction itself. We've known several people who went through this—they didn't have a way forward—and couldn't see past the problem (the addiction).

You might be wondering what is wrong with focusing on the problem. After all, wouldn't focusing on the addiction be important to overcoming it? What's wrong with that . . . it seems normal?

But imagine how an addict feels when all their attention is focused on their addiction. Chances are, they're weighed down and miserable—the very state they're trying to escape. Think about how you feel when you are focused on a problem. Usually, you feel weighed down by it. Hope seems to evaporate the more you focus on it. Negative energy surrounds the problem.

Which is precisely why the *problem* is exactly the *wrong* place to start.

When we began training managers and leaders on how to develop and execute a plan, as mentioned earlier in our research, we noticed that most people and organizations did very little planning. When most managers would try to develop a plan, almost across the board they used the *problem* as the starting point—which is exactly backward when using the Six-Step Process. It's difficult to go from problem to solution and be highly successful.

Most people fall into the trap of relying on gut-level reactions. We're often told to trust our guts, and while that's good advice in many situations, making decisions about complex issues isn't one of them. Willy-nilly decisions don't yield great outcomes no matter how many fingers you cross.

Worse, some people allow their emotions to get ahead of their gut (especially when starting with the problem), unable to connect with the smart parts of their intuition. They end up flying blind, pursuing one course, then shifting to another, all with no clue about where they are. Are they moving toward their target? Away from it? They may get lucky after shooting from their metaphorical hip, but too often, reactionary decisions put them, and their organizations, back at square one, or worse.

Maybe you've felt this way at some point. Remember, it's not just you. This is human nature. It's how most humans are wired to deal with things. The good news is that it probably isn't your fault, just as, in another situation and organization, a similar result due to lack of a clear process might not be the fault of a manager or team member. For most people and leaders, nobody has taught them a better way and so they are doing the best they can with the information they have.

That's where the Six-Step Process comes in and why we are so confident that it will transform your life, your family, and your team. Without further ado, let us introduce the Six Steps and get into how you can use them to start impacting your organization and life today:

The Six-Step Process:

1. WHAT IS THE VISION/GOAL?

2. WHAT IS THE CURRENT REALITY?

3. IDENTIFY THE REAL ISSUE.

4. WHAT ARE THE BEST OPTIONS?

5. DEVELOP AND IMPLEMENT THE PLAN.

6. DEBRIEF AND EVALUATE RESULTS.

As an introduction to the process, let's see an example that most people can relate to in one way or another. Even in this brief example, you will quickly see how you can approach any issue differently from how the masses do.

Imagine that one morning you are looking at your body in the mirror and you think to yourself, "I want to look and feel better. I feel overweight, low on energy, and out-of-shape. I need to do something to change and get healthier."

Sound familiar? If not, you surely know someone who has felt that way.

We've identified the problem. Now, how would you go about solving it?

With no process to guide you, default human nature takes over. The responses and reactions we just discussed will manifest themselves.

You might set a New Year's Resolution hoping your health gets better. Or, maybe you go a step further and say, "Next week,

I'm going to start exercising and eating healthier; then I'll begin to lose weight and I won't feel so tired."

Can you already sense what's wrong here? Thinking this way jumps from the problem ("I'm unhealthy and out of shape") directly to the so-called solution ("I'll become healthy and get in shape"), completely ignoring what comes in between. That rarely, if ever, works. This is why approximately 85 percent of New Year's Resolutions are broken by January 15th!

Without a clear plan, nothing changes.

Start with the Vision

When you take the Transformation Challenge and use the Six-Step Process, you always start with the vision. In other words, you identify your desired outcome first. It seems counterintuitive because the problem is the thing you want to resolve. The problem might have been the reason—the pain point—that gets your attention and brings you to the table of wanting to change.

Remember: When you focus on the problem, you're putting yourself and/or your team into a place of negative energy. When discussion centers on the problem, finding positive solutions becomes hard, if not impossible. Inevitably, you start looking for what's wrong, and almost without realizing it, you get stuck mulling over everything that's wrong with the situation—it's the antithesis to being solution focused.

For the moment, set aside the current, looming problem and ask yourself, "What end result am I looking for?" Your mental reality will precede the physical reality.

Looking back to Lydie's case, she had spent years thinking about all the reasons why she *couldn't* build a school in Rwanda. She was focused on the problem. This effect becomes magnified within a team because focusing on the problem can devolve into a complaint session, which isn't productive and leaves morale low and the climate unsatisfying.

As you lead your life or team, successful leaders shift the playing field from the problem to the vision. The vision changes the entire tone and feeling.

So, back to our scenario: you want to look and feel healthier. Let's see how focusing on the problem tends to poison the well.

If you constantly think about how overweight you are, the low energy, and fatigue, you may not even realize that you are letting your thoughts wallow into a stagnate pool of negative energy. These thoughts act like parasites, draining your enthusiasm to change and your belief in your ability to improve. Generally, it's hard to escape from that type of place. What a depressing thought!

In this scenario, what if you started with the vision *to feel healthy, vibrant, and full of energy*? With just a few words, can you already feel a difference? Simply by shifting the problem (being low on energy and overweight) to the vision (being healthy, vibrant, and full of energy), *everything* has shifted. The entire feeling is different. Imagine how that amplifies within a team scenario.

Once you can articulate your vision—your destination—you can use the additional steps of the Six-Step Process to help you establish a clear way forward and a detailed plan to get there. When you apply the remainder of the Six-Step Process, it stokes excitement and hope.

Though the Six-Step Process is not the first problem-solving process, it is one designed to solve *any* problem or address any opportunity you encounter. True, it started as a methodology specifically for those in businesses and organizations. But we found it can be applied just as effectively to your personal world as it can to an organization.

We have spent years researching other planning processes and nothing else we've seen is so versatile, simple, or powerful in achieving true results.

One process we encountered is called Six Sigma, which drives lean, high-quality manufacturing. Six Sigma is so specific to a certain area that trying to apply it to a variety of scenarios would be almost impossible. Could you imagine trying to apply Six

Sigma to the previous health example? How many people do you know who would do that? For us, the answer is nobody!

The Six-Step Process is a one-stop-shop that you can apply to any circumstance. Think of it as the universal process that fits any problem, challenge, or opportunity. It can be used in the most complex business scenarios or in helping a child develop a plan for success.

The Six-Step Process immediately gives you a positive place to start. *What is the vision?* The remaining steps give you a clear and logical path to achieve your vision by finding outstanding solutions, developing a specific plan, and evaluating results along the way.

Are you ready to get started?

In the next chapter, you'll get to meet a woman who was on the verge of losing a billion-dollar company; a couple whose marriage seemed to be drifting apart; a friend who was unemployed for eighteen months and wondering how to break through and get a job; and a woman whose sales business wasn't earning the money she needed.

Although we could have used exclusively business examples, we decided to share examples from a wide swath of backgrounds to illustrate the versatility of the Six-Step Process. We hope that you will be able to resonate with at least a couple of these scenarios or that they might feel familiar to you as you relate them to your life or team.

In that spirit, as you read about the real-life examples and case studies, think about your challenges or opportunities that you wrote down earlier. Ultimately this is about *you* and helping *you* achieve *your* best, whether personally or doing this as a team. Remember, it's called the Transformation Challenge for a reason. The Six-Step Process will help you transform any issue you use it with.

If you haven't already done it, you can visit www.TheTransformationChallenge.com to download a Free Six-Step Process Quick Start Guide. You can use this free template as you read the remainder of the book.

All right . . . let's get started!

CHAPTER 2

Stories from the Field: Five Case Studies

Facts. Figures. Stats. These form the foundation and frame of knowledge. Beyond percentages and numbers, however, humans tend to learn most effectively through stories.

Stories capture principles and processes in action. It's easier for most people to relate to a principle or process when looking through a self-introspective lens at someone else's story.

In this chapter, we will examine five real-world examples of people who applied the principles of the Transformation Challenge and used the Six-Step Process to achieve big results.

Although there are numerous examples of organizations that use the Six-Step Process, we want to illustrate how versatile the process is by also sharing some personal and relationship examples.

We hope that you will share these stories—and The Transformation Challenge—with a friend, co-worker, or family member who you feel would benefit from the Six Steps in their life or business.

A Challenged Marriage

Ben and Lisa met in college many years ago. They quickly became good friends and enjoyed spending time together.

Ben had even said, "Whoever Lisa ends up marrying will be one lucky guy!"

One night, they were both at a dance party and Ben asked Lisa to dance. Lisa was a phenomenal dancer. Ben, however, had two left feet. It was a bit like Ginger Rogers trying to fox-trot with Frankenstein.

Despite Ben's awkwardness, however, he felt playful and at ease with Lisa. And it was during that dance that a light bulb ignited in Ben's mind. He realized that Lisa was not only beautiful and fun to be with, but she might be *the one* for him!

They began dating and saw each other every day. A year later, during their senior year of college, they married. Lisa was twenty, and Ben was twenty-three.

Their early years of marriage were like Camelot. They loved being together and going on adventures. They loved hiking, skiing, and being outdoors together. They also loved spending quiet nights at home, just being together.

Ben started a successful career in business. After a few years, they had their first child. Circumstances allowed Lisa to fulfill her dream of staying home to raise their children as a full-time mother. Over the next fifteen years, they welcomed two more children to the family.

In the early days of their growing family, Ben and Lisa devoted much time to each other. They loved being together, loved each other, and loved each child that came into their lives. But gradually, as the children grew, Ben and Lisa became so busy with work, kids, and life that it felt like they rarely saw each other anymore.

Lisa felt more like a taxi service than a mother or wife as she ferried her kids to soccer and football games, dance classes, and piano lessons. Ben was the tag-team partner who worked hard all day and came home to take kids to the activities that Lisa couldn't cover. Nearly every evening and weekend was booked, pulling the family in different directions. Ben and Lisa had to divide and conquer. What they didn't count on, however, was that their relationship was slowly and imperceptibly dividing—and being conquered.

One day, they were driving—and alone! They found themselves enjoying a rare, private conversation, the kind that used to be the foundation of their early days of dating, marriage, and parenthood. Now, in a quiet moment together, they reflected on their long marriage. They both came to the same shocking conclusion.

They realized that they spent almost no time with each other anymore. It was as though they were living two independent lives. Some days, their only time to connect was when they prayed together in the evening before bed. The fun and romance of their Camelot days had faded. And they were so busy, they never saw it coming.

They had heard stories of people getting divorced after being married for twenty or thirty years—something that had once seemed unfathomable to them. But now, it didn't seem so farfetched. Although they both agreed that they didn't have an unhappy marriage, they realized that they needed to make a course correction to avoid their own divorce after decades of marriage.

Ben and Lisa still loved each other. Yet the gravity holding them in orbit to each other had weakened and they were slowly drifting apart. How had this happened?

As they became hyper-focused on their work and their children, they no longer devoted time to each other. They no longer cultivated the fire they had sparked long ago. That fire that had once been a roaring inferno; now it had faded to embers.

They both cared deeply about their family and Ben's business success. And, they knew that they wanted to stoke those flames between them once again. They committed to doing better. Good wasn't good enough. They wanted great.

They both knew, too, that it wouldn't just happen for them because they had talked about it. It would take effort. Focused effort. They needed a plan. Otherwise they would be leaving their relationship to fate, merely hoping things would get better on their own.

Hope and wishful thinking alone wasn't going to change anything.

If you were a partner in this marriage and you felt what was happening, how would *you* approach it? How would you make the necessary course correction—and how would you develop an exciting, actionable plan to improve the marriage—without getting into an argument?

Flying J

As a kid in the 1950s, Jay Call had grown up around his father's gas station. He loved it. In fact, he loved it so much that in his early twenties, he tried his hand at running one himself, taking over a station from his father. He excelled at it.

In 1968, he officially launched his own business, calling it Flying J, based on his dual passions of flying and ranching. He began with four small discount stations, but it wasn't long before Flying J expanded into California and the Northwest. He eventually took the concept of the gas station and evolved to a full-service travel plaza.

The first Flying J travel plaza opened in 1979 in Ogden, Utah. Jay kept innovating and expanding, revolutionizing the trucking throughout the eighties. By 2009, Forbes had ranked Flying J thirteenth on its list of the largest privately held companies in the United States, and the company was one of the leading travel centers in the country.

Steve first met Jay back in 1982, through an international organization of business leaders. Jay had a lovely and smart teenage daughter named Crystal. Then and now, she's a light to anyone who knows her. We enjoyed watching her develop into a successful businessperson herself.

Crystal grew up learning about the family business from her dad. One of the most important lessons she learned was the importance of treating the employees of the company as part of the family.

As she constantly observed and learned from her father. She took stock of what worked and what didn't, and developed her own entrepreneurial skills and spirit. Following in her father's footsteps, Crystal started her own business: The Crystal Inn Hotel Group.

As time passed and Crystal had her own growing family, she remained actively involved with Crystal Inn Hotels, while serving on the board of directors of Flying J. They were on top of the world and the future looked brighter than it ever had.

Tragedy struck in March 2003 when Crystal's beloved father was killed in an aircraft accident. Jay had been flying friends to their home in Sun Valley, Idaho, and everyone on the flight perished when the Cessna Citation mysteriously went down.

Jay's sudden passing left a gaping hole in Crystal's life. She had lost her father, trusted mentor, and business partner. Jay Call's influence, spirit, and legacy will forever be a part of Crystal's life, but losing him was devastating.

Despite the loss and its emotional aftermath, Crystal still had to tend to an avalanche of details and tasks—both as daughter and as a Flying J board member—that required her immediate attention. Flying J continued to grow and generate tremendous financial success. By 2008, Flying J had surpassed $18 billion in revenue.

But not long after hitting that milestone, in early 2009, the Flying J board of directors discovered that Flying J was facing a dire financial crisis. There was a multi-million dollar cash shortage with no way to raise the funds necessary.

How had this happened?

It didn't take long to track down the cause. It hinged on two key decisions made by the company's previous president and CEO—decisions based on the price of oil.

First, Flying J bought and remodeled an old oil refinery. Second, the company purchased a pipeline from the Gulf of Mexico to Dallas, Texas. The goal was to give Flying J a significant market advantage by eliminating the middle man in their supply chain. Oil prices were soaring and it seemed like a wise investment. Flying J put $1 billion at stake for these purchases— and the entire venture relied on oil prices that were high and constantly trending upward.

Had the market for oil remained high, these investments might have paid off as intended. But the market dove and the price of oil plummeted.

The impact was beyond devastating. It put Flying J's very existence in jeopardy.

Within a short time, Flying J faced a $400 million operational shortfall. The company had already tapped out its financing to purchase the refinery and the pipeline. The CFO didn't mince words: without a line of credit or a source of capital, Flying J would be no more. All that Jay Call and his family had built would be lost.

The president and CEO responsible for this had been at the helm of the company for almost twenty years. Although the company remained successful throughout most of his tenure, he had failed to keep the board apprised of the looming financial disaster.

The board turned to Crystal for guidance. She and the president met in January 2009. As they discussed strategies for solving the crisis, it was clear that they didn't see eye to eye.

Because Crystal and her brother were the largest stockholders of Flying J, and because of her background as a successful business person, the board appointed her as the new president and CEO with the hope that she would pull off a miracle.

It seemed an impossible task. No matter how much Crystal pondered, brainstormed, and strategized, she didn't see a way out.

The banks called in the notes. Gloom contaminated the company at every level. Everyone was discouraged and bracing themselves for the moment when the company—and their jobs—would be lost.

Crystal felt it was her responsibility to find a way to save the business, its employees, and everything her father had spent his life building. Jay, Crystal, and the Call family had always seen their employees as the most valuable part of their businesses and cared for them as family. She couldn't let them down. The crushing weight of the responsibility kept her up most nights.

Despite her determination and resolve, many people around Crystal told her that it would be impossible to save the company.

What would you do if you were in Crystal's shoes? How would it feel to be responsible for a family of employees when nearly everyone is telling you that saving the company—your father's legacy—is impossible? Where would you begin?

Shawn and the Eighteen Months of Unemployment

Shawn was forty-eight. He led a team responsible for the advertising, marketing, and promotion of a very successful kitchen and bathroom remodeling company. Skilled, energetic, dedicated, and talented, Shawn felt that he was on top of his game.

Over the course of five years, he gave the company his all. He spearheaded several projects, including organizing and attending shows and conferences, creating promotional exhibits, and creating successful ads for print, radio, and television. But when the company reorganized the marketing department to cut costs, Shawn got laid off.

At first Shawn wasn't too worried. With his skills in promoting and building businesses paired with his successful marketing ideas, he anticipated that there would be a bidding war for his services. What company *wouldn't* want him?

Feeling optimistic, he applied for various jobs. But as his jobless days turned into jobless months, he began to worry.

The job market was extremely tight. Despite Shawn's talent, he still couldn't find a job after eighteen fruitless, grinding months of applications, interviews, and networking. It eroded his confidence and chipped away at his self-esteem. If it hadn't settled in already, depression wasn't far off.

Haunting questions tormented him. He began doubting his abilities, skills, and the impact he could make in an organization. He felt deeply discouraged at his prospects of finding a meaningful job that paid him what he was worth. Worse, guilt plagued him because he was failing to financially support his family.

Shawn wasn't the only one feeling this way. Being out of work for so long exerted immense tectonic pressure on the once immovable plates of his marriage and family. His unemployment quickly became the ten-thousand-pound elephant in the room, affecting the quality of his family relationships.

His wife had to take on extra work. Bills piled up. They had trouble affording things the kids needed. Shawn worried what others thought of him, including his children, extended family, and friends. He tried to stay positive, but the discouragement soon permeated every aspect of his daily life. With every tick of the clock, he felt more isolated, alone, and powerless.

How you would feel if you were in Shawn's shoes? How would you get your life back on track, emotionally and professionally, after a blow like this?

A Business with a Broken Process and Millions of Dollars on the Line

Eagle Systems International is a company of around five hundred employees that is an industry leader in providing general efficiency services, from residential to commercial. Over the years, they've earned the trust of utility companies and hundreds of thousands of customers.

Eagle has seven different divisional offices, each with an experienced group of senior leaders and managers. The employees and executives work hard to be among the best in class, because the company's reputation for quality, customer satisfaction, safety, and reliability are critical to its success.

Just a few years ago, Eagle was a service provider for a large public utility company—one of the best gas and electric public utilities in the country.

Eagle was contracted to fulfill several programs for the utility. One of their biggest programs was for helping low-income customers. Eagle would contact qualifying customers and perform an energy audit of their home or apartment. Based on the audit, Eagle would then upgrade the lighting systems, repair or retrofit heating and air-conditioning units, install energy-efficient refrigerators, and make sure they had sufficient insulation. When Eagle was finished with each unit, they would submit an invoice with all the supporting documentation to the utility.

All the programs that Eagle ran for the utility had very high customer satisfaction ratings. All but one. The management team running the Energy Audit program was causing some serious headaches for the utility company. It was getting so bad, it was jeopardizing the business relationship between the two companies.

The problem was this: the utility regularly received non-compliant notices for the energy audits performed. According to regulations, each audit required a customer signature on the qualifying paperwork within five business days, and the Eagle team running this program were out of compliance.

Eagle's history of commitment to customer service and program success was among the best in the industry, and yet things were quickly going downhill in this relationship. Palpable tension tainted the interactions between the teams involved. Further, it endangered the million-dollar contract for this low-income program and threatened to cause irreparable harm to the two companies long-term business relationship. To say Eagle was gravely concerned would be an understatement.

Imagine now that you are the leader of Eagle. You know the problem: Eagle is clearly out of compliance because they aren't processing the required paperwork within five days. Nobody on your team has any ideas for solving the issue. Frustration grows as hope fades. How would you revitalize the team and figure out a way forward to solve this compliance issue?

Starting as a Partner or Distributor in a Direct Sales Business

Kate had been a successful manager throughout her life in several different organizations. In her late forties, after leaving her previous company, she decided to try her hand at starting her own business and building her own direct sales team.

She became a distributor in a large direct sales company. Excited and enthusiastic, Kate jumped into her new business venture.

Yet after a few months her excitement faded. Others in the organization had instructed her to simply "find her why, develop a plan, and go to work." Yet, she quickly learned that it wasn't that simple. She wasn't sure *how* to develop a plan or *how* to "go to work."

Soon, doubt crept in, undermining her resolve. Could she really be successful in this industry? Deep down she felt like she could be successful in direct sales, if only she could figure out the next steps she needed to take.

Have you ever been in a situation like Kate's—not sure where to start or how to move forward?

After attending a BYB conference, Kate became one of our executive coaching clients and showed up for a one-on-one coaching session. She was hopeful that we could help when she frustratingly described her current situation; if you were in our shoes, how would you coach her and help her develop a specific plan to achieve her dreams and goals?

How about You?

These are just a few examples of real people facing real situations, all in very different circumstances. In the upcoming chapters, we'll revisit these case studies so you can see how each person took the Transformation Challenge and used the Six-Step Process to alter their course and transform their reality. (Spoiler alert! They all found hope and created solutions where it appeared that none existed.)

Now, it's time to think about *you* and *your* happiness, success, and prosperity, whether using the Six-Step Process for you or with your team. Think about the change, big issues or opportunities in your life—remember, you wrote them down earlier.

For your first time through the Transformation Challenge, simply choose *one* of these challenges, problems or issues. This will be the issue you apply the Six-Step Process to. Each chapter will describe a step in the process, and at the end of each chapter, you should apply the lessons outlined to your specific issue.

By the end of the book, you will have gone through the entire Six-Step Process, and you will be amazed at how powerful it truly is. It will give you a clear plan that will open doors you thought were locked and knock down obstacles you thought were invincible. This is *your* case study, and we're excited to see where you go.

CHAPTER 3

Step One:
What Is the Vision and Goal?

Imagine this: you're the manager of a team and sales have been declining for the past five months. How would you respond? Most managers in this situation might call a meeting and go right at the problem. *Why have sales been declining for the past five months?*

Here's a different situation. Let's say that you discover that a son or daughter crept out at night to experiment with drugs for the first time. How might you respond? Most parents would probably lose it and go straight at the problem like a guided missile. *We can't trust you anymore! Why did you sneak out to do drugs?*

As we mentioned in the previous chapter, the *problem* is the exact *wrong* place to start. Instead, the most successful people and leaders shift the playing field from the *problem* to the *vision*. The vision is the right place to start.

Think about the difference between those two starting points. What kind of energy emanates from the problem? It's typically negative, contentious, and poisonous to effective solutions. On the other hand, what kind of energy pulsates from the vision? It's radiant with positive energy. It's uplifting, inspiring, hopeful, and a place where solutions seem to organically bloom. The vision is an empowering place to start, but in today's world the most common response is to go straight to the problem.

This is the reason the Transformation Challenge starts focusing on the vision and *not* the problem!

So, what is the vision exactly? It is the high-level desired outcome. The vision is *not* a goal because it doesn't need to be specific or measurable (that comes later). The vision is a focus beyond the obstacles and doubts and seeing *where* you want to be. That's precisely why the vision is exciting. It drives you, and it gets other people involved and aligned (when working with a team).

When we facilitate a planning and execution workshop for an organization, participants often ask us, "Should I be using our company vision to start the Six-Step Process, or should I develop a vision for this particular issue?" In this case, the answer is usually to develop a vision for whatever issue you chose for the Transformation Challenge. Whether you use the Six-Step Process as a company, a team, in a marriage, or personally, the vision should apply to the specific issue that you are trying to improve.

With that in mind, let's revisit the declining sales scenario at the beginning of the chapter. We imagined that a manager might start with the problem by calling a meeting to figure out why sales have been declining for the past five months and then try to figure out how to fix it. Suppose, however, that this manager applies the Six-Step Process to the challenge instead of using the standard gut response. Rather than the problem of declining sales, the first step would be to determine the vision for the sales team.

While it's true that the company or team may have an overall vision for the company or department, in this case, our manager should form an issue-specific vision. In our scenario, the manager might come up with this vision: *To be a part of a great team and have a record sales year.* He or she may even refine it after discussing it with the team: *Have an outstanding sales team that surpasses our sales goals and is the premier sales team in the entire organization.*

Can you feel the difference in that approach? Which manager would you rather work with? The manager who starts the meeting with, "All right, sales have been declining and it needs to stop. We need to figure this out and reverse the trend." or "All right team, our vision is: *To have an outstanding sales team that surpasses our sales goals and is the premier sales team in the entire organization.* Now, over the past five months . . ." When you start with the vision, it takes your eyes beyond the obstacles and focuses them on the exhilaration of the finish line. In this case, instead of starting with the problem, the manager has established the vision or the high-level desired outcome for this issue. This immediately paints the picture of the desired direction for the team.

Now let's revisit the second scenario where you discover that your child has sneaked out of the house at night to go dabble in drugs. How you handle this situation could be a critical juncture in your relationship that will have an impact for years to come. As a parent, you might be tempted to start yelling, ground your son or daughter, or ask them, "Why would you do such a thing? Don't you know the impact this will have on your life? I can't believe you would violate our trust!" In the emotion of the moment, this can certainly be difficult to shift the playing field to the vision and thoughtfully walk through the Six-Step Process. So, what vision would you formulate before sitting down with your child to talk?

One option would be *to have an outstanding relationship with John or Jill.* Or, *to have a high-trust relationship where we can count on each other to tell the truth through thick and thin.*

This immediately changes the tone of the coming discussion, transporting parent and child to a place of hope and positive energy! As you will see in the upcoming steps, you aren't ignoring the issue or the problem, you're simply shifting the starting point of the discussion to the vision.

....

What is the goal (if necessary)?

This part of Step One takes practice. The vision is the very first step and it is the *high-level* description of what you want to accomplish, do, or become. Once the vision is established you *might* need to define a specific goal as part of the plan.

However, that is not *always* the case. Sometimes we may not have all the information necessary to establish a clear goal or objective. Other times, you might have plenty of information, and the goal or objective is the key piece of the puzzle to develop an actionable plan to accomplish the vision. Each situation is different. But when a goal is necessary, it is critical that it be worded the right way.

According to our research, did you know you are 90 percent more likely to accomplish something when you have a clearly written goal and plan? Yet, on average, only 10 percent of people have clearly written goals. Isn't that an amazing irony? You are 90 percent more likely to accomplish something when you have a clearly written goal and plan, yet only 1 in 10 people do it.

Interestingly, we have found that this skill set of how to set goals is rarely taught in college at either the undergraduate or even the graduate level. You might be amazed at how many managers and executives struggle to come up with clearly written, actionable goals that are worded correctly and effectively drive a behavior. In most cases, it isn't their fault, they just haven't been taught how to do it. However, this is a skill set that can be learned by anyone. It simply requires someone to show them how, and then practice doing it repeatedly.

The reason why the correct wording in the goal is so important is so you can develop a clear plan around the goal. Why do most New Year's Resolutions fail? Because they aren't worded correctly. For example, the two words you should almost never use in a goal are *more* and *better*. In addition, the goal should almost always be kept to one sentence.

Many people and teams unknowingly set themselves up for failure the moment they write their "goal." So, let's briefly review how to write a goal the correct way so that it is clear and specific—and actionable.

SMART Goals

This is one of the keys to effective goal setting—and, in our experience, one of the hardest areas to get right.

As we mentioned, we have worked with CEOs, managers, and leaders who typically struggle with this in the beginning. As with all skills, however, the more practice they get, the easier it becomes. We have heard people say, "I used to set what I thought were goals, but now I realize that I was actually setting our team up for failure because of the way we wrote the goal, and that's why I didn't get the outcomes I was hoping for." Words are important!

Goals become SMART goals when they are Specific, Measurable, Achievable, Relevant, and Time Specific:

SPECIFIC: The more specific the goal, the more likely you are to achieve it. With that in mind, which of these examples do you think is better?

(1) *Lose more weight and eat better*

(2) *Be at 135 pounds by October 30th*

Of course, the second example is better because it is more specific and easier to develop a plan to accomplish. Yet, we have seen the first example used countless times at all levels of business and in people's personal lives. If a person was to use the first example as their goal, the truth is that most likely nothing would change in their life.

Furthermore, the second example is phrased in a positive way. Positive goals feel more achievable and are more motivating than negative ones. Notice in the example we didn't say *lose fifteen pounds*; instead we put a target weight. The more specific you are, the better.

MEASURABLE: You should be able to look back at your goals and objectively say "Yes, I did," or "No, I didn't," accomplish them. A measurable goal increases accountability and is more likely to motivate you to accomplish it. As we mentioned above, rarely use the words "more" or "better" in a goal. Compose the goal so that it's measurable.

Here is another real example of a non-measurable versus a measurable goal:

(1) *Have a great relationship with my spouse*
(2) *Go on at least two dates a month without the children*

The second example is a better goal because it is measurable. The first example is a nice vision, but a poor goal because it is neither specific nor measurable. The first example allows for a lot of wiggle room, but the second example will cause you to be accountable because it is either a yes-no goal. Yes, I took my significant other on two kid-free dates this month; or, No, I did not take my significant other on two dates this month.

ACHIEVABLE: While your goals should stretch you and maybe even take you outside your comfort zone, they should still be achievable. If you are a sophomore in college with only $1,000 in your account, it may not be realistic to set a goal of earning $10 million in the next six months. If your goal is unachievable or even just too difficult, a person is more likely to be discouraged and give up. A goal should generally stretch you enough to make you feel slightly uncomfortable.

RELEVANT: Your goals should be relevant to your vision. If a part of your vision is, *I am a healthy and well-rounded person*, then relevant goals would tie in with health and exercise such as: *Run a half marathon in less than two hours by September 20th.*

TIME-SPECIFIC: If possible, add a date or time to your goals. For example: *Finish a 5K in less than twenty-eight minutes by July 21st*; or the one we used earlier: *Go on at least two dates a month without the children.* When there is a time or date element attached to the goal, it further increases your accountability.

If your goal is SMART, you've overcome the hurdle that trips up most people and teams.

Fighter pilots, in addition to mastering air combat, also master the art of goal writing. Why? Because their lives depend on it. They brief to the goal, they fly to accomplish the goal, and they debrief to the goal. In the world of fighter pilots, it's all about achieving the vision and goal. The good news is that you don't have to be a fighter pilot to practice and get great at composing SMART goals. Start with the vision and then develop a clearly written goal when necessary.

We've said the phrase, "when necessary" a couple of times. As you take the Transformation Challenge, there are instances when you will only have a vision, because you may not be able to set a clearly written goal yet. For example, if you are planning a family vacation in the coming year, the vision might be *To have an incredible and memorable family vacation.* You may not have a goal yet—just the vision as a starting point. If that's all you have, that's okay.

Another example might be if you have a flawed product and you are trying to figure out the flaw. The vision might be *To deliver an outstanding product to the customer that is bug-free.* That would be a great starting point for the vision, but maybe you don't have enough information yet to develop a SMART goal. So, you simply start with the vision.

If a goal is useful as you start the planning process, one caveat to keep in mind is to only have one goal per plan. So, back to the declining sales scenario, if the vision is to *Have an outstanding sales team that surpasses our sales goals and is the premier sales team in the entire organization*, then the SMART goal for this plan might be *Pass at least $2,000,000 in sales by March 28th*. That is a single goal that supports the vision, especially if it would stretch the team and really help them be the premier sales team. What we wouldn't do is set a multi-component goal to *Pass at least $2,000,000 in sales by March 28th, increase customer satisfaction by 4 percent, and decrease turnover by 8 percent*. Now there's way too much drawing attention away from the primary goal. In that example, each of those goals should be its own Six-Step Process.

The key is to start the Transformation Challenge with the vision, and—when necessary—a SMART goal. It's the right starting point that shifts the entire conversation.

Let's return to our case studies to see how each began their Six-Step Process by defining their vision in their own lives and organizations.

CASE STUDIES—STEP #1:
WHAT IS THE VISION/GOAL?

A Challenged Marriage

If you'll remember, this story involves a couple that has been married for almost twenty years. One day while they were driving they reflected on their marriage and realized that they hardly spent time with each other anymore, and they were really living two independent lives. They knew they needed to make some course corrections to avoid a path that potentially led to divorce.

During their two-hour drive, they decided to take the Transformation Challenge with their marriage and use the Six-Step Process to develop a plan. Like most people, they were tempted to start with the problem: *We don't see each other very often and our relationship isn't what it used to be—we're so busy it's like we each have our own life and are drifting further apart.*

This couple, however, resisted that inclination and instead, using Step One of the Six Steps shifted the playing field from the problem to the vision.

They asked themselves, "What is our vision as a couple? In other words, what do we want our marriage to be like in ten or twenty years from now?" Discussing their vision gave them a chance to talk about things that would get them excited about their marriage and bring a fire back to their relationship. Simply talking about their vision was a powerful exercise for them as they realized they hadn't had that type of discussion for more than a decade.

In this case, the vision they came up with for Step One was this: *To have an outstanding marriage filled with passion, excitement, love, and fun memories together.* Would that vision get you excited if we were talking about your marriage? For us, absolutely!

In this case, they didn't feel like they needed to set a goal or objective. They simply wanted to make that vision a reality. They were ready for Step Two: What is the Current Reality?

Flying J

In this story, everything seemed to be going well at Flying J, until one day the CFO came to our friend Crystal and told her, "Crystal, we're out of money. Not only are we out of money, but if we don't come up with $400 million in the next 30 days, then we're done."

Whoa! Could you imagine being in her shoes? What would you do? There were literally thousands of people counting on Crystal to steer the company in the right direction so that they could support themselves and earn an income.

Crystal shared the dire news with some of her closest advisers to see if they had any ideas or solutions, and they all told her the same thing: "There's no way to save the company." Many of them advocated for her to file Chapter 7 bankruptcy and shut Flying J's doors forever.

This was truly one of those times that exemplified the saying, it's lonely at the top. Would Crystal listen to her advisers and close the doors? Or would she discover another solution that potentially could save the company?

Fortunately, Crystal chose the latter option, and she went to work seeking solutions. She called her team together and shifted the playing field from the problem to the vision. What do you think her vision was in this scenario?

You probably guessed it. It was *Save the company!* That is simple, clear, and it is a great starting point. Most people would have called a meeting and started with the problem. "All right, we have $400 million in debt, the morale in the company is low, people think they're going to lose their jobs. How do we solve this?" For this team, the vision was a great starting point because it catalyzed positive energy and brought life back to the team. The vision was the exact *right* place to start and it brought a burst of life and energy to the team that maybe there was a solution.

What's more, in Crystal's case, it was appropriate to set a goal to accomplish the vision. Her goal was *Come up with $400 million in the next 30 days.* It was a specific, measurable, and a solid goal that they could build a plan around.

Now that the vision and goal were clear, the team could move forward in finding solutions. They were ready for Step Two: What is the Current Reality? From a place of hope and excitement, her team was ready to rally and help her accomplish her goal and fulfill her vision.

Shawn and the Eighteen Months of Unemployment

In this example, Shawn the forty-eight-year-old husband and father, had been laid off. Even though Shawn was very talented and capable, over a period of eighteen months and numerous interviews, he still couldn't find a job.

As you can imagine, he was discouraged, frustrated, and his self-esteem had taken a real hit. This was a low point in his life, and it was having an impact on his health, family, and marriage.

As part of a humanitarian fundraiser, he and his family decided to do a 5K run with our family. I (Steve) asked Shawn if, rather than run the race, he would be willing to walk with me and use the time to take the Transformation Challenge to see if it could help him find a job.

He was game, and so we started walking on a brisk November morning. I asked about his situation, and like most people, he sprinted right at the problem. He started telling me about the job market and the impact it was having on his family. It was time to shift the conversation.

I asked him what his vision was for this situation. He responded, "I want to provide for my family and put food on the table." I laughed and told him, "Okay, that's a start, but that's not a quite the vision we're looking for. Let's raise the bar to something that really gets you excited and passionate!"

He started tossing out some more ideas, and as he continued to talk, he started to get more and more excited about his *real* vision. Ultimately, he settled on a vision that revved his motivation and filled him with enthusiasm. It was to *Help the owners of my new company sleep well at night and get a job that allows me to spend high-quality time with my family, helps me achieve my financial dreams, and helps me feel excited when I wake up in the morning.*

Obvious question: Is that a different feel than his original suggestion of *Provide for my family and put food on the table*?

By this point in our walk, he was already fired up and felt a sense of hope that he hadn't felt in a very long time. In this case, he didn't know what the goal would be, so we decided to stick with the vision and go to Step Two. Imagine the difference he felt by starting with the vision, rather than the problem!

A Business with a Broken Process and Millions of Dollars on the Line

Here, we were following the plight of Eagle Systems, an energy efficiency service provider. They have numerous contracts and programs with several utility companies. They had several programs that they were running for a single, large, public utility. On most of the programs, Eagle maintained a great relationship with the utility. However, there was one program that was causing headaches for both sides. The longer the misalignment lasted, the more tension built between Eagle and the utility's program manager.

The problem centered on paperwork. When Eagle finished a job, they were supposed to submit paperwork within five days. Eagle's teams, however, were consistently three or four days late. This was particularly odd for Eagle, which in every other team and area delivered service at the highest level of quality.

The Eagle team that was consistently submitting late paperwork decided to take the Transformation Challenge and use the Six-Step Process to transform this deteriorating situation. The stakes were high; it had the potential to cost the company millions and an invaluable long-term relationship with the utility.

For Step One, they sat down as a team and rather than focus on the problem—non-compliance to submitting official paperwork—they started with the vision. After a short discussion, they decided that in this situation their vision was to *Help the utility deliver a highly successful program with a high-trust relationship and be in compliance 100 percent of the time.*

As in our previous examples, this team grounded themselves in the vision, fostering hope, excitement, and strategic thinking.

In this case, they developed a goal: *Finalize a compliance plan within the next thirty days that gets reporting to less than five days.* The goal was SMART, and it supported the vision. Now they were ready for Step Two of the Six Step Process: What Is the Current Reality?

Starting as a Partner or Distributor in a Direct Sales Business

In our final case study, Karen had launched into the direct sales world as a partner/distributor for a large company. Initially, she was thrilled and excited for this new venture. However, her enthusiasm quickly faded as she realized she didn't have a plan and it seemed daunting to start her own team—especially after several people told her *no.* She was wondering if she really had what it takes.

In April, she attended the Becoming Your Best (BYB) Breakthrough Leadership Conference and decided to invest in personal coaching with BYB. When we sat down together, she explained her excitement and frustration. This was the perfect opportunity for her to take the Transformation Challenge and use the Six Steps.

When we initially asked her what her vision was in this arena, her response was, "To have a better life!" That might sound like a vision, but it is *not* a vision. She fell in the trap that many people and teams fall into—setting the bar too low in their description of the vision. We asked her to think big and raise the bar. "What would really get you excited? Describe that future for us."

Ultimately, after some discussion, we settled on the following vision: *To be financially independent with a strong passive income and have the freedom of time to do what matters most in her life.* She was excited and enthusiastic about that! After talking about her current income and a few other factors, we decided to help her set a goal in conjunction with her vision in Step One. Her goal became *To achieve a gold rank by April 1st* (about four months away).

When she started the conversation, she was initially focused on the problems and all the reasons why it was hard for her. After identifying her vision and a goal, there was a palpable excitement in the air and she felt the initial enthusiasm come surging back. She had successfully set the stage for Step Two.

YOU DO:

Now it is time for you to take the Transformation Challenge and apply Step One of the Six-Step Process to a real-world issue in your life or with your team. It doesn't matter whether the issue is part of your personal life, a relationship, or an organization.

Remember, the vision should be simple, clear, and inspiring. If it involves a team, everyone should feel buy-in. Don't set the bar too low. When you read the vision, you should feel excited, aligned, and inspired by hope! Also, remember that a goal isn't always necessary if you don't have enough information to make it a SMART goal. Sometimes you may just start with the vision. If you do decide that a goal is relevant for you, however, only use one goal and make it SMART.

WHAT IS THE VISION?

_____

_____

_____

_____

WHAT IS THE GOAL (IF NECESSARY)?

_____

_____

_____

_____

IF THERE ARE OTHERS INVOLVED, DO THEY UNDERSTAND THE VISION/GOAL? _____

PROCEED TO STEP #2: WHAT IS THE CURRENT REALITY?

CHAPTER 4

Step Two:
What Is the Current Reality?

Analyzing the *current reality* helps you determine whether you or your team are achieving your vision and goal or are on track to achieve it. This may seem simple, but it can be quite challenging.

For example, in the days before the global financial crisis of 2008, how many banks were aware of the *real* situation and sensed the problem in time to take corrective action? This was to be the worst financial crisis in decades, but few, if any, understood the current financial reality.

In a marriage, one partner may feel like everything is perfectly fine and not perceive the current reality that their partner quietly yearns for a divorce—much to their partner's surprise!

The current reality describes the state of the issue *today*; it is a snapshot of the issue this very moment. As you assess your current reality, be thoughtful, considerate, yet brutally honest. Try to be as objective as possible. Pretend you are the bird on the window sill looking in on the situation with total objectivity. What do you see? Emotions can be part of the current reality, however, use caution to not let emotion cloud the facts. Stick to the facts as objectively as possible.

If you're doing this as a team or with your organization, you may need to compile some data so that you can accurately assess the current reality. Remember, you are describing the situation as it looks and feels *today*.

Once you identify the current reality, then you simply determine whether there's a *gap* between your vision and the current reality. If so, then you move to Step Three. If your current reality already matches the vision, there isn't any reason to go to the next step. In other words, if the current reality matches the vision—you are already there!

To illustrate this process, let's look at a simple relationship example. In this example, a long-time couple has begun the Six-Step Process. After establishing their vision, they are ready to analyze their current reality.

VISION:

- **Have a happy, exciting, and close relationship filled with great memories!**

CURRENT REALITY:

- **We have no meaningful dialogue or talks between us anymore.**
- **We go on a date every two or three months.**
- **We do not see a lot of laughter between us anymore.**
- **We are both busy, busy, busy in different areas of life.**
- **We've been together for years and have a lot of fun memories.**

- **We have two kids who we love and want to see succeed.**
- **We treat each other civilly and are respectful of one another.**

After outlining the points of their reality, the couple determines that there is clearly a gulf separating the vision from the current reality. So, the partners would move on to Step Three and identify *why* there is a gap between the current reality and the vision.

Not to get ahead of ourselves, but you can't develop a plan unless you know the root cause (why) for the gap separating the current reality and vision. This is one of the reasons the Six Steps are so powerful. In this situation, most couples would start with the problem and go right to the solution phase. *We don't talk anymore or spend time together. How do we fix it?* That approach rarely helps the situation improve.

Let's look at another example of analyzing the current reality. Here, we'll revisit the sales team from the previous chapter. If you'll remember, their issue was declining sales for several consecutive months.

VISION:

- **Be the premiere sales team in North America that crushes our yearly target and is a fun, exciting place to be each day.**

CURRENT REALITY **(constructed from the insights of the team and compiled real data):**

- **Sales have declined by 12 percent in the past 90 days.**
- **At the current sales pace, we will miss our annual target by at least 18 percent.**
- **We have an amazing team of people who are hard-working, dedicated, and loyal to each other.**

- **This product (or service) has been on the market for six years with no adjustments or modifications.**
- **Morale has been a little low in the past couple of months because of declining sales.**
- **We have full support from the management team to make recommendations and develop a new sales plan.**

As an organization, if your vision and current reality don't match, it is critical that you move to Step Three and identify *why* there is a gap.

Do you feel the power in starting with the vision, and then assessing your reality with total objectivity? As we have mentioned several times, most people would go directly from problem to solution, missing these critical steps. It's difficult to solve a problem if you don't first understand the vision and where you currently are today.

Now, let's rejoin the people in our case studies to see how they assessed their current realities. See if you can relate their stories to your own situation.

A Challenged Marriage

After focusing on the vision, Ben and Lisa were already feeling excited about the direction of their conversation. Together, they developed and refined the vision: *To have an outstanding marriage filled with passion, excitement, love, and fun memories together.*

Now, it was time for them to objectively assess the current reality. How do things stand for us today? Below are a few things they came up with as part of the current reality:

- **We love each other and have many fun memories together.**
- **There is a feeling that each person has become so busy with different things in their individual lives, that it seems like we don't talk a whole lot anymore.**

- **It's been more than 45 days since our last date.**
- **We don't see each other very often—maybe only a few minutes in the morning and the evening.**
- **We have three talented children who are involved in numerous different activities.**
- **We're less intimate than we used to be.**
- **We don't plan our weeks together anymore.**
- **We both have a desire to rekindle the fire and bring back a great feeling to the relationship.**

As you can see, their current reality didn't match their vision. Their current reality is a snapshot of how they perceive their relationship as it stands *today*. So, before they could develop a plan to achieve the vision, they would first need to identify *why* there is a gap between the current reality and the vision. Without identifying the root cause of the vision gap, their plan would potentially solve the wrong issue. Ben and Lisa were ready for Step Three.

Flying J

This highly successful company was number 17 on the Forbes Largest Private Companies List in the United States. That was when they discovered that they had a $400,000,000 cash shortfall. Total corporate failure seemed imminent. They enlisted Crystal as the new CEO, longtime member of the board and daughter of the company's late founder.

What was the vision? *Save the company!*

The goal was to *Come up with $400 million in the next thirty days.*

Crystal brought her team together to assess the current reality. They compiled data so that they had an accurate picture of what the current reality *really* was. Because of the size of the company, there were a lot of data points that came out as part of that discussion.

What did their current reality look like? Here are some of the points that comprised their assessment:

- **The banks had called their loans and they had a $400,000,000 shortfall of cash.**
- **Their core business was in travel centers and truck stops. In fact, the travel centers and truck stops were still highly profitable.**
- **In recent years, they had branched out into buying a petroleum refinery and a pipeline.**
- **They had purchased the oil for their refinery and pipeline at $800,000,000 and now the price of oil had dropped significantly.**
- **Flying J had 16,000 employees and payroll was coming up.**
- **Most people were saying that the company couldn't be saved, and they would have to close their doors.**

These and other points that they outlined showed that there was a giant gap between Flying J's vision to *save the company* and their current reality. They were in serious trouble, and it looked like closing their doors might be unavoidable. It was time for them to identify the root cause for the gap and develop a plan to save the company!

Shawn and the Eighteen Months of Unemployment

During our walk together, I asked Shawn about the current reality. He commented that he used to be a successful marketing and IT pro, but after numerous job interviews and no offers he was discouraged, his self-esteem was low, and there was a real friction developing at home because of the financial pressures.

He paused for a moment as he considered his new vision: *Help the owners of my new company sleep well at night and get a job that allows me to spend high-quality time with my family, helps me achieve my financial dreams, and helps me feel excited when I wake up in the morning.* Then together we really took stock of his current reality. Here are some of the points he listed:

- **He had been unemployed for eighteen months.**
- **He had six different job interviews, yet none of them offered a follow-up interview.**
- **Shawn was a large man at 6 feet 3 inches, 250 pounds, a shaved head, and a hunter's beard. He was 47 years old (notice this is simply an objective observation). In other words, he may appear intimidating to some people.**
- **Shawn had an excellent track record of skills and accomplishments, especially in marketing, IT, and human relations.**
- **The unemployment rate in his State was 4.5 percent.**
- **They were living on his wife's income alone. There was an increasing financial shortfall in their family's budget.**

In Shawn's case, there was clearly a gap between his current reality and his vision. He wasn't even close to achieving his vision at this point. He was ready to go to Step Three and identify the root cause of the gap.

A Business with a Broken Process and Millions of Dollars on the Line

Matt, one of the talented managers at Eagle, led the discussion to address the big issue harming Eagle's relationship with the large public utility. The team developed the vision to *Help the utility deliver a highly successful program with a high-trust relationship and be "in compliance" 100 percent of the time.* They formulated a goal based on this vision: *Finalize a compliance plan within the next thirty days that gets reporting to less than five days.* In other words, 100 percent of the jobs would be successfully submitted within the five-day deadline.

With this vision and goal clearly in mind, Matt and the team articulated the current reality:

- **This program was regularly out of compliance with reporting times between eight or nine days—the expectation was five.**
- **Eagle received daily messages from the utility for being out of compliance.**
- **The utility expressed constant negative comments about Eagle's performance on this program, and there was a real risk those negative feelings and frustrations could impact other programs that Eagle was successfully running for the utility.**
- **Eagle was recognized as an industry leader in service and in almost every instance delivered impeccable quality.**
- **They had a group of very talented employees, but no current process in place to meet the five-day turnaround on paperwork required by the utility.**

Between the vision and the current reality, the Eagle team saw a large gap. Therefore, the next stop for Matt and the team was to go to Step Three and identify the real root cause of the gap. With millions of dollars on the line, you'll be surprised to see how this entire scenario transformed in the upcoming steps.

Starting as a Partner or Distributor in a Direct Sales Business

During our coaching visit, Karen was fired up about her vision and goal. Her vision was *To be financially independent with a strong passive income and have the freedom of time to do what matters most.* She brimmed with excitement and enthusiasm at the very thought of her vision! Then, she formulated the goal: *Achieve a gold rank by April 1st* (approximately four months away).

We asked her to describe the current reality while we wrote her answers on a white board. This is what she came up with:

- **She had started out filled with enthusiasm, but lost her confidence after talking with several people who told her *no*.**
- **Although people told her to develop a plan and follow the plan, she really didn't know where to start (which made the *no's* that much more daunting); therefore, she didn't have a specific plan.**
- **She loved the product, but was having very limited success up to this point.**
- **She didn't have a professional Facebook page or website set up.**
- **She had a lot of family, friends, and other people who she hadn't approached yet because she lost her confidence.**
- **She knew it was possible to be successful because she personally knew other people who did well.**

Diagnosis? There was a gap between her current reality and vision. Just as in the other case studies, Karen needed to go to Step Three and identify the root cause of the gap. Once she identified that root cause, *then* we could develop a plan to effectively transform her situation and start getting the results she wanted.

What Does This Step Mean to You?

There is true power in starting with the vision—and when necessary a goal—and then clearly identifying the current reality. If there is a gap, then a person or team moves to Step Three, *Identify the Real Issue,* to determine the root cause of *why* the current reality doesn't match the vision.

As we've pointed out several times, human nature drives most people to go directly from the problem to the solution and then wonder why nothing changes. You are now armed with a simple process that you can use repeatedly, either personally or in your organization.

Now, when you develop a plan, you will have a clear sense of direction (your vision) and an accurate assessment of where you are (the current reality). When that happens, you will be better equipped to navigate change and create a specific plan to achieve your desired results.

For many, taking the Transformation Challenge and going through the Six-Step Process will bring a hope and excitement they haven't felt for a long time. It kindles optimism and enthusiasm to reframe the problem in the context of the vision and then assess the current reality in relation to the vision.

By this point, you should have already developed a vision for the issue you chose as part of the Transformation Challenge. Now, you can assess the current reality. Be as objective as possible and compile the necessary data when working with a team.

YOU DO:

CURRENT REALITY:

1.

2.

3.

4.

5.

6.

7.

8.

9.

10.

CHAPTER 5

Step Three:
Identify the REAL Issue

Many of you reading this book might remember the tragic Space Shuttle *Challenger* accident on January 28th, 1986.

Challenger was the second in the shuttle program after *Columbia*. It had successfully completed nine missions in three years. Then, seventy-three seconds after its tenth lift-off, *Challenger* exploded as it streaked toward space. All seven crew members were killed.

So, let me ask you this: Why did the Space Shuttle *Challenger* explode?

If you are like most of the participants in our seminars, then you answered, "Because the O-ring failed."

While that is correct, it is important to remember that the O-ring failure wasn't the *real* issue—the root cause of the tragedy. It was only a symptom of the real issue. So, if it wasn't the O-ring, what was the root cause?

In the *The Toyota Way: 14 Management Principles from the World's Greatest Manufacturer*, one of the best studies on root cause analysis, Jeffrey K. Liker suggests asking the question *why* at least five times to dig down to the true root cause of an issue.

If we follow that advice in the case of *Challenger*, we should ask *why* several more times.

Why did the O-ring fail? Because the temperatures were so cold that morning that it caused the O-ring to freeze and ultimately fail.

Why didn't someone speak up if they knew there was a possibility of the O-ring freezing and failing? Someone did speak up, but nobody would listen to them because of the intense public pressure to launch the shuttle.

Why wouldn't anybody listen to the engineers that tried to stop the launch? Because the engineers didn't have a vote in the decision to launch or delay the shuttle.

Why didn't the engineers have a vote decision in the launch process? Because there wasn't an adequate Go/No Go process in place to halt a launch, no matter what, if the required conditions weren't met.

At last, we have arrived at the real issue—the root cause of the *Challenger* tragedy. The O-ring failure was just a symptom of the absence of a Go/No Go process. Had the team investigating the tragedy stopped asking *why* after getting their first answer, they would have never identified the real issue.

Imagine that alternate reality for a moment. The investigators proclaim that the O-ring was the culprit. NASA replaces all the O-rings with O-rings that must pass stringent new manufacturing checks before installation. Everyone thinks the problem is solved. But in another launch, the engineers are now worried about another part of the machinery: the propellant valves. But since they still have no adequate Go/No Go process, the engineers can't halt the launch. NASA could be heading for another disaster, even though they fixed the O-rings; they failed to fix the root cause.

Fortunately, the investigation unearthed the root cause of the disaster. Now NASA has a tremendous Go/No Go process. Now, there are numerous people throughout the launch process who have the authority to stop the launch.

There is something else to consider about Step Three: Identify the REAL Issue. This concept is one of the most important that we cover in this book. **If you are using the Six-Step Process to address a problem or issue that has already happened**, Step Three may be the most critical of the Six Steps. If you don't identify the *real issue* that is causing the gap between the current reality and the vision, you may develop a great plan—but it won't solve the root cause of the gap. **On the other hand, if you are using the Six Steps to plan something for the future**, this step may not be as relevant for you. Let us explain with a couple of examples.

Suppose that your vision is to *Be in shape, healthy, and feel great about your body*. However, your current reality is that you feel overweight, unhealthy, tired, and out of energy. Clearly, a gap stands between your current reality and your vision. In this example, you are dealing with a real-time issue that has already happened: you've gotten out of shape. Therefore, Step Three is extremely important because you need to determine the root cause of the gap between the current reality and your vision. If you don't, your plan will most likely fail because it never addresses the real issue causing the gap.

Now suppose that you are using the Six-Step Process to plan a family vacation. Your vision is *Have a wonderful and safe family vacation filled with great memories together*. Your current reality is that you're excited as a family, but you really haven't started the planning. In this example, you are dealing with an event that hasn't happened yet: going on a future vacation. Therefore, Step Three will not be as relevant to your planning. This will be true in most cases when applying the Six-Step Process to a future goal or aspiration.

The reason for this is that the gap between current reality and vision is simple. When we're planning for a future goal or event, we don't have enough data to determine root causes. The event hasn't happened, therefore there can be no root cause analysis to tell us why your current approach may not be working.

That doesn't mean to skip Step Three altogether if you're working on a future goal. It can still be a useful exercise. But remember, Step Three is indispensable if you're attempting to transform an issue or state of existence that has already occurred.

As you search for your root cause, be aware of primary factors and contributing factors. In the fighter pilot world, whenever an accident occurs, authorities convene an accident investigation board. The board has thirty days to answer the question: *Why did the plane crash?* The investigators will often identify one or two *primary* factors that caused the accident and several *contributing* factors.

As you search for the root cause of the gap between your or your organization's current reality and vision, you'll probably find one or two *primary* factors and several other contributing factors.

In digging for a root cause, you're trying to discover the *primary* reason(s) for the vision gap in your situation. If you continue asking *why*, the contributing factors will lead you to the real issue. One of the common mistakes in doing this is that people stop asking *why* too soon. They identify one or two contributing factors and think they've discovered the real issue. Keep digging. Keep asking why. That's how you will unearth the primary issue. If you are using the Six Steps for a personal issue, sometimes the *why* can be painful and it's not easy to go there. However, if you hope to make something better in your life, you need to be willing to look at uncomfortable truths—it's one of the only ways to make it better is to expose the issue and develop a plan to address it.

With that context in mind, let's revisit our case studies to see how Step Three unfolded for each of them.

A Challenged Marriage

Ben and Lisa's vision was to *Have an outstanding marriage filled with passion, excitement, love, and fun memories together.* They had a good marriage, but there was clearly a gap between their current reality and the vision. They started asking *why*. And they didn't stop until they excavated the root cause.

Here's what they came up with:

Why don't we spend enough time together? We're busy with Ben's travel and because the kids are so busy in their different activities, we don't take the time to plan for each other anymore.

Why don't we take time to plan for each other anymore? Because we don't allocate the time on Sunday to plan our weeks together anymore.

Why don't we plan our week together before the week starts? Because neither of us have been doing our own individual pre-week planning anymore, nor do we have any goals as a couple.

Why don't we do our individual pre-week planning anymore? Because we both had paper planners at one point, and when the year that was in the planner finished, we didn't get new planners. Because of that, we slipped out of the habit and stopped doing our pre-week planning.

In this case, Ben and Lisa felt like the real issue holding them back was that because they were so busy, they had individually stopped doing their pre-week planning. Since they didn't do it individually, they certainly didn't sit down at the beginning of the week to plan their week together. In other words, they were just winging it. They had devolved to living a life by default rather than a life by design. How many times does this happen to you or someone you know?

This was a big "Aha!" moment for them. Many years ago, when they were young in their marriage, Ben and Lisa each did their own pre-week planning. Then they would sit as a couple on Sunday evening and go through each day of the week together, making time to be together. Every week, they would schedule time for each other! They did this for years, but once they slipped out of that habit, the marriage began its barely perceptible slide. They drifted apart slowly, but steadily.

Before going through Step Three, Ben and Lisa thought that the root cause of their drifting relationship was that they were so busy. It wasn't—although it is true that they were living hectic, busy lives. The real issue was that they simply didn't plan their weeks together anymore, which resulted in them spending little to no time together. But it took them asking why multiple times to uncover the root cause. With the root cause identified, they can go to the next step and develop ideas and solutions to address the real issue and start moving toward their vision.

Flying J

During the company's financial crisis, Crystal shared her vision with her fellow executives to *Save the Company!* Their current reality showed that they were at real risk of losing the company. Crystal and the executive team moved forward to understand the *real issue* causing the gap between the current reality and the vision.

It was obvious that there was a $400M shortfall of cash. The question they had to answer was, *why was there a $400M shortfall?* One of the reasons was that Flying J had invested several hundred million dollars into an oil refinery. This refinery was several decades old and required another large investment of $200M to bring it up to date.

Why did they invest in the refinery? To allow Flying J to be in greater control of the end product and to better control pricing.

Was the oil refinery necessary for the profitable operation of their core business of travel centers and service stations? No.

Again, why did they invest in the refinery? Nobody had a good answer for that final question. It was clearly outside the core competency of Flying J.

They didn't let that single answer stop them, however. They continued digging. *Why else was there a gap?* They also recently invested several hundred million in hundreds of miles of oil pipeline to bring oil in from the Gulf to a central distribution point. More importantly the supply of oil in the pipeline had an initial value of $800M.

Why did they invest in the pipeline in the first place? The intent was to reduce transportation costs for the oil and to be more competitive. Yet the gambit came at a significant risk because of the volatile oil market. If oil prices maintained a reasonable market value, they could get a strong return on their investment. Unfortunately for Flying J, oil prices experienced a sudden and sharp drop, which caused an immediate cash shortage and crisis.

These factors, precipitated by the investments in the oil refinery and pipeline, were the direct causes for the $400M cash shortage. Crystal and the executive team examined the data, and it was clear that the travel centers and other business units were performing exceptionally well. She asked if the travel centers could continue to sustain profitability on a long-term basis without the refinery and pipeline. The answer was a resounding yes. However, travel centers and other business units could not produce enough short-term cash to solve the problem.

As Crystal and the other key executives continued to ask *why* and how they had gotten into this situation, it became apparent that the previous long-time CEO had made these decisions without the Board's knowledge or consent, putting the company in a high-risk position if the price of oil dropped. With greater transparency into the previous CEO's decisions, this risk position could have possibly been avoided and the strategy changed.

Crystal and her team determined that the root cause of their predicament was the unilateral actions of the previous CEO, who had landed Flying J in a high-risk venture that was completely beyond their core competency of service stations and truck stops.

Now that they had identified the real issue—investing in businesses outside their core competency—they could go to work developing a plan to address that issue and save the company.

Shawn and the Eighteen Months of Unemployment

Shawn was very well qualified and had an outstanding track record of past employment. On our 5K walk together, I asked him *Why wasn't he able to get a job after eighteen months?* He answered that he didn't have a bachelor's degree and therefore could not list this on his résumé.

This is a good place to pause and point out that the lack of a degree is simply a contributing factor to the root cause; it's not the primary reason, although Shawn felt like it was the primary reason. He commented that in today's digital world, if you don't have a bachelor's degree your application is automatically kicked out of the pool of applicants. This reduces the number of initial job interview opportunities.

Why else haven't you been able to get a job after eighteen months? Shawn felt that the interviews he got didn't go well.

Why didn't they go well? He would freeze up during the interview process and the interviewers couldn't see the real, fun-loving, capable Shawn.

Why would you freeze up? After so long of being unemployed he had lost his confidence and even started questioning his own abilities and skills.

Why did he feel like he lost some of his abilities, especially during the interview process? Because he hadn't practiced or role played with anyone prior to his interviews, so he got extremely nervous and would forget what to say.

Great! We just identified one of the primary issues: he wasn't practicing and his interview skills had really deteriorated.

Is that all? Why else does this gap exist? Because Shawn was a larger man with a shaved head and mountain-man beard, his appearance may have intimidated the interviewers.

Why might his appearance potentially scare the interviewer? Perhaps the interviewers thought that this physically imposing, gruff-looking man could potentially initiate violence in the workplace; or perhaps that he would bully his co-workers when things didn't go his way.

As we dug deeper by asking *why,* we discovered the real issues: Two main factors with one contributing factor.

PRIMARY FACTOR 1. His interview skills had deteriorated significantly because he didn't practice or role play.

PRIMARY FACTOR 2. The first impression he made could be perceived as intimidating.

CONTRIBUTING FACTOR. His applications were weeded out due to his lack of a degree.

There were several other contributing issues, but they weren't strongly related to the primary issues.

Armed with this type of clarity, Shawn was excited and anxious to move on to the next step in the Six-Step Process. Fortunately, we still had two kilometers to go in our 5K walk. This was going to be one of the most monumental and productive 5K's we had ever participated in. ☺

A Business with a Broken Process and Millions of Dollars on the Line

Matt from Eagle brought the team together to analyze why there was a gap between their vision (*Help the utility deliver a highly successful program with a high-trust relationship and be in compliance 100 percent of the time*) and the current reality.

Matt started off with the first question: *Why are we out of compliance?* One reason was that the paperwork needed to be sent to the company's regional office for input, quality assurance, and accuracy review. It could take up to two days for the outreach representative to get the paperwork in the mail; by the time the regional office received the paperwork, it was already day four.

Why was the paperwork being mailed from the field rather than being done electronically? The team had no answer other than, "That's how we've always done it."

What else is at play here? If it can take up to four days just to get the paperwork to the office, why is the paperwork being sent to the utility nine or ten days late? Once the paperwork arrived at the Eagle office, it could take another 48 hours to process it and get it back in the mail to the utility. By that time, it was already day seven, eight, or nine—and WAY out of compliance.

Why is this paperwork taking so long to process? They didn't have a local office for this program so it was sent in the mail rather than delivered by hand.

Why isn't there a local office? Because the program should justify and pay for itself, it needed to be viable and sustainable, as well as efficiently run with a high confidence of meeting the utility requirements.

After this root-cause analysis, they determined that the *real issue* causing the gap was having to mail the paperwork from the field to the office for review, and having to mail the paperwork again from the office to the utility. As fast as Eagle's team was, there simply weren't enough days to get it all complete within the compliance-mandated 5-day window. Therefore, the primary issue in this case was a broken process due to office location and mailing time.

They were excited to move to the next step because they were certain they could come up with winning solutions and ultimately realize the vision!

Starting as a Partner or Distributor in a Direct Sales Business

Karen was excited about her vision (*Be financially independent with a strong passive income and have the freedom of time to do what matters most*) and her goal (*Be at the gold rank by April 1st*).

However, there was a clear gap between here current reality and her vision.

During our coaching visit, I asked her, *Why do you feel like there's a gap?* She responded that while she initially felt excited and optimistic, she felt like she had stalled out.

Why do you feel like you've stalled out? She was busy, and she was discouraged because a few people told her 'no;' therefore she was no longer doing any type of income-producing activity. Clearly there was a lot going on in her response. I decided to choose one of the three things she had mentioned—the one that she had total control over.

Why aren't you doing any type of income-producing activity? When she got started, she reached out to family and a couple of close friends and that was it. She figured that was about as far as she would need to go for her business to take off, so she didn't really have a plan after that (especially when her initial contacts turned her down).

Why haven't you developed a plan? Her response was that she had simply been too busy, but the truth was that she didn't really know how to develop a plan.

Being busy and discouraged were *contributing* factors, but they weren't the real issue. The primary issue was that she didn't have a detailed plan. As the maxim states, when a person fails to plan, they plan to fail. This was a big "Aha!" moment for her when she realized that without a plan, she was simply winging it and most likely destined for failure.

It was time to move to the next step in the Six-Step Process and help her come up with some options, develop a plan, and help her accomplish her vision.

What Does This Step Mean to You?

Why is Step Three so important in this process? If you're addressing an issue that has already happened or is currently happening, it is critical you identify the *real issue* that is causing the gap between your current reality and vision. Once you identify the real issue that is causing the gap, you can develop ideas and solutions that solve the *real* issue and help you achieve long-term, winning results!

YOU DO:

Identify the Real Issue causing the gap between your vision and current reality:

WHY?

_____

_____

_____

WHY?

_____

_____

_____

WHY?

_____

_____

_____

WHY?

_____

_____

_____

WHY?

_____

_____

_____

CHAPTER 6

Step Four:
What Are the Best Options?

The door to the room is closed and locked. The key executives for Flying J sit around a table as Crystal explains that the vision is to *Save the company*!

They have dug down and unearthed the root cause that created their $400 million shortfall crisis: they veered from their core competency and invested in an oil refinery and a pipeline. Crystal says to the group, "Today, we are not going to leave this room until we can come up with a viable plan to save the company. We have an incredible team and the best professional resources available to help us. Let's go to work and come up with the best options to save the company." The executive team rolls up their sleeves and goes to work!

The example of Crystal in this situation shows us how a great leader can be even more effective when they use the Six-Step Process to transform issues. Think about what most other leaders might have done in Crystal's situation. Many would gather their team, state the problem (starting with negative energy), and then start working on ideas to solve it (without knowing the root cause). They would miss the key steps of starting with the vision, assessing where things currently are, and identifying the real issue.

Because of the insights and revelations of the first three steps, Step Four of the Six-Step Process, *What Are the Best Options?* is perhaps the most exciting. Why? Because you have fostered a positive mind-set to unleash your imagination and find solutions— even if others may say there are none to be found. Remember, the preparation leading up to this step will make a huge difference in the quality of the outcomes and options that you generate.

So, how do you come up with the best options, exactly? What will unleash your creative juices and spawn a big list of possible actions and ideas to solve the issue? Two of the most powerful ways to fan the flames of imagination are brainstorming and mind-mapping.

Let's start with brainstorming. For optimal, *effective* brainstorming, take one or two minutes (before you start the brainstorm) to review what you came up with in the first three steps of the process: the Vision, the Current Reality/Gap, and the Real Issue(s). Make sure you and/or your team, clearly understand each.

The Rules of Positive Brainstorming

1. Appoint a team leader and a scribe. It's helpful to have a leader who can keep things moving and a scribe who can take notes while others participate in the discussion.

2. Set a manageable group size of 2–8 people. If you have more than eight people, then some of the group will generally stop sharing their opinions and ideas.

3. Take a minute or two and discuss how to maximize the number of ideas. Sometimes it's nice to go around the circle and after one person shares an idea, go to the next person. If the next person doesn't have an idea, they can say, "pass." Another way to do it is to have a free-for-all. Whoever has an idea can shout it out. A brainstorm is all about *quantity* of ideas, not *quality*. This is the idea generation phase. The team leader shouldn't allow anyone to criticize others' ideas. You can foster idea creation when you say something like "great idea" after a person shares their idea.

4. During the brainstorm, go for quantity, not quality. Remember, a brainstorm is about idea creation. You will sort through the ideas later for quality, so at this point, just focus on quantity. Let your brain run free. The old saying is true while brainstorming, "There are no bad ideas!"

5. Don't develop a plan yet. One of the most common mistakes we see when working with organizations is that they will get a good idea that hijacks the brainstorm session. This happens because they start to develop the plan around that idea rather than continue with idea creation. Do not stop to debate or decide if the ideas make sense or not. You are not developing the plan at this stage, you are only coming up with possible ideas and solutions.

6. Set a time limit of a between ten minutes to an hour. Generally, you can generate some great ideas in just ten to twenty minutes. This will vary with the complexity of the problem or opportunity. For very complex issues, this type of brainstorming could take multiple sessions over the next few days or weeks. Explain to the group that you will prioritize the ideas when the brainstorming phase is complete.

7. Sort through the list for quality. After you feel like you have most of the ideas on the table, this is when you switch modes from *quantity* to *quality*. With your team, you can discuss and debate which ideas are the best. Which will have the greatest impact in realizing the vision? If you are working on a personal issue on your own, sift through your ideas to identify the best ones. You can do that by identifying the pros and cons to each idea—which ideas have the most pros and the least cons? Once you've discussed and decided, rank the selected ideas from highest to lowest in terms of anticipated impact.

8. Are the ideas ethical and feasible? After you've sorted through the ideas and ranked them, you need to make sure that each option is both ethical and feasible. Strike those that are not from your list. You are almost ready for Step Five!

Brainstorming is a powerful way to generate ideas. Sometimes a brainstorm will happen organically, and other times it will help to schedule a formal brainstorm with your team—just like Crystal did with her team at Flying J. Now, let's look at another approach: mind-mapping.

How many times have you felt like you were tapped out of creativity and your well of ideas had run dry? Mind-mapping can jump-start the brain just when you think your idea generator is totally drained.

From another angle, how many times have you said or heard someone say, "I'm just not a creative person," as an excuse for not coming up with ideas. Thomas Edison famously said, "Genius is 1 percent inspiration and 99 percent perspiration." For Edison, creativity was a *work* thing. When you purposefully make time for yourself to be creative, and go to work at it, that's when the ideas come.

Mind-mapping is a powerful way to activate parts of your brain that would otherwise remain dormant. It's a great way to unleash ideas at any time, but especially after you've hit the wall and are ready to call it quits.

How to Mind-Map

1. Choose the central idea, problem, or vision and put it in the center of the page.

2. Branch out from the center and write an idea, and from that idea, write another. You're allowing your brain to connect ideas with other ideas. You will almost certainly come up with ideas that you hadn't thought about before. It might look something like this when you are finished mind-mapping ideas:

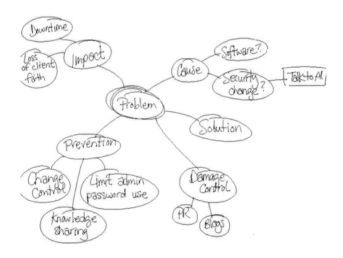

3. Don't stop! We were with a Fortune 500 company and one of their leaders chose a big issue to mind-map. He had never done mind-mapping before in his life. He started the process and then after about two minutes he put down his pen. I looked at him and asked him to keep going and see what other ideas he could come up with.

A couple of minutes later he gasped and said in a loud voice, "I just came up with an incredible idea!" After everyone else was done, he commented to the group that this was his biggest "Aha!" of the day. His best idea came *after* he thought he was finished. This is not uncommon. So, when you think you're done, consider going just a little further and you may surprise yourself.

4. Highlight the best ideas. Once you're finished, highlight the best ideas and rank them from top to bottom in terms of impact. Just as in brainstorming, ask whether each idea is ethical and feasible. Strike those from the list that are not.

Even though it may appear a simple technique, most leaders and employees we've trained have never done any type of mind-mapping. They are often amazed at the amount of ideas they can generate in this relatively short activity and the impact those ideas have on their results.

Brainstorming and mind-mapping are just two ways to unlock your imagination and flush out ideas that otherwise may have never have surfaced.

GO/NO GO!

After you've developed a list of feasible, ethical ideas that will help you realize your vision, pause and assess whether your plan is a Go or No Go. *If* your ideas and solutions will solve the real issue and close the gap between the current reality and the vision, then you are a *Go*. If you decide that none of these ideas will help you address the real issue and achieve the vision, you're looking at a *No Go*.

It's like orienting your map with a compass and taking a bearing of the landscape. If the compass points you in the wrong direction, you're a No Go. If you find yourself staring in the face of a No Go, repeat the brainstorming process and continue looking for ideas or solutions.

Be on heightened watch for No Go's if you are using the Six-Step Process to move toward a *future* goal or opportunity. The following example demonstrates why.

A company hired us to conduct a planning workshop with their key executives as they were preparing to launch a new division. Prior to launch, they wanted to initiate a pilot program that would cost $2 million to pilot. The company was all in and ready to invest in the proposed pilot.

The executive team proceeded through the first four steps of the Six-Step Process. When it was time to decide Go/No Go, all the executives agreed: it was crystal clear that this was a *No Go*. They realized that if they were to divert their time and attention away from their core business, it could have catastrophic results. They couldn't believe it. In less than two hours, the Six-Step Process had helped them save $2 million dollars that they would have surely lost in the pilot. Those two hours were certainly worth their investment of time and energy to save them all the pain and expenses they would have faced because of the failed pilot!

What's interesting about this example is that this organization is like most organizations. They were going to throw a bunch of money at a challenge/opportunity without a clear plan just hoping that it works. How many times have you had that happen to you or someone you know? It was only when they used the Six-Step Process that the path forward illuminated with a clear direction—in this example, No Go.

Let's drop in on our case studies to see what ideas they came up with and whether it was a Go or No Go.

A Challenged Marriage

After getting to the root cause of the issue, Ben and Lisa went to work brainstorming ideas that they felt would address the issue and help them achieve their new vision. Below are a few of their ideas:

1. **Start doing individual pre-week planning and take 30 minutes Sunday evening to plan our week together.**
2. **Go on two dates a month without the children. Alternate who plans each date.**
3. **Within the next thirty days, sit down together and develop annual goals as a couple. This will help give us something to work toward together.**
4. **Go on at least two fun weekend trips alone before the end of the year.**
5. **When we are home together, take at least five minutes to read together and talk to each other about the day.**
6. **No electronics in the room after 8:30 p.m.**

There were a few more things on their list, but you get the idea. As they reviewed their list of ideas, they both felt an excitement surge back into their relationship. They suddenly felt like they were in control again and weren't just hoping things improved.

In retrospect, these might look like simple or obvious solutions. *Why didn't we think of this before?* you might wonder. Remember, the Six-Step Process clarifies the situation and converts good intentions into reality. It will help you develop a vision and then sort through the clutter to reveal the root cause of what's preventing you from achieving your vision. These ideas didn't just appear out of nowhere. Steps one through three tilled the ground and planted the seeds.

Ben and Lisa were again creating a relationship by design rather than a relationship by default. They prioritized this list, and then asked if these actions would help them achieve their vision and change their current reality. They both agreed that the answer was a resounding yes! It was time to move to Step Five and turn these ideas into a specific plan.

Flying J

At the beginning of this chapter, we joined Crystal in a locked room with her team of executives. She was determined to stay in that room until they had viable ideas that would help them achieve the vision . . . *Save the company!*

After they finished a careful review of the real issues revealed in Step Three, they started the brainstorming process. Throughout the day the team came up with many options and ideas to save the company. From the long list, they narrowed it down to fifteen important actions that would restore the company and keep it going. We've included just a few of them here:

1. **Seek protection under Chapter 11 Bankruptcy. This move would provide the time needed, under bankruptcy supervision, to do the things that were required to save the company.**
2. **Sell the oil refinery.**
3. **Divest Flying J of the pipeline.**
4. **Consider some type of merger or strong financial partner for the travel center/truck stop part of the business. This would provide an added source of cash.**
5. **Develop a clear communication plan to ensure all employees understand the plan so that there were no rumors or misunderstandings about the demise of the company.**

At the end of the day, the Flying J team prioritized their ideas from top to bottom, with the most critical and important actions first on the list. As they sat back and analyzed what they had accomplished, they all agreed: this was a Go.

Just as important, the atmosphere of gloom and doom that had so recently contaminated the executive team was swept away and replaced with excitement, confidence, and a tremendous focus to move forward. What's more, it wasn't just the executive team that felt this new hope. That same positive attitude quickly spread throughout the entire organization. Flying J had the foundation for a bold and very strong restructuring plan in place, and they were ready to move to Step Five: Develop and Implement the Plan. What most had considered impossible, was now very possible!

Shawn and the Eighteen Months of Unemployment

As Shawn reflected on the discussion that we had during our 5K walk, he was inspired and energized. His journey through the first three steps had helped him to see the issue clearly. Now that we had identified the root cause of the gap, it was time for the real fun—what could he do to make his vision a reality as soon as possible? We started brainstorming together. A few of the ideas we came up with were to—

1. **Revise his résumé to include his Bachelor of Arts in LE (Life Experience). ☺ This would get him through the computer filters that were automatically kicking his résumé out of their system.**
2. **Consider his appearance, and take measures to appear less intimidating at first appearance. In this case, the idea was specifically to shave his burly goatee. Once people knew Shawn, they would quickly discover that he has one of the most kind and considerate hearts in the world. This idea was all about the first impression.**

3. **Practice and role play the employment interview. It was Friday and he had another interview coming up on Monday.**
4. **Anticipate and practice every possible question that could come up in the interview so that he could remain calm, cool, and collected.**
5. **Carefully research the company that he had an interview with on Monday. Be sure it was one that was compatible with his vision and one where he felt like he could make a difference.**
6. **"Chair-fly" the actual interview, visualizing a successful outcome. Chair-flying describes closing your eyes, visualizing the scenario, and mentally practicing the interview ahead of time.**

These were a few of the ideas we came up with together. As Shawn reviewed this list of ideas, we prioritized them and put them in order. For the first time in a long time, Shawn was excited and felt a surge of hope. He had a clear focus that was a definite, high-fiving *Go*. He was ready for Step Five—to articulate the actual plan of *who* will do *what by when*.

A Business with a Broken Process and Millions of Dollars on the Line

With his team at Eagle, Matt reviewed the vision and the current reality. It was clear that there was a major gap between them. They needed a five-day turnaround to get documents to the utility, however they were currently doing it in eight-plus days.

After a careful analytical review of *why*, it became clear that the current process would never be able to deliver acceptable results due to the logistics of multiple mailings.

During Step Four, the team had a great brainstorm to develop ideas that would help solve this problem. Here are a few of their ideas:

1. Consider processing the paperwork electronically versus a paper-based system. In other words, create a software program and get portable devices for the technicians that would allow them to submit all paperwork electronically rather than using mail.
2. Consider an electronic signature versus a paper-based "wet" signature.
3. Open a small office closer to the utility's main office. This would put them in closer proximity, allow them to improve their service with other programs, and possibly reduce travel costs.

Even during the short brainstorm, the team was pumped up about these ideas. They were also amazed that nobody had ever thought about making the shift from paper to electronic. It was a seemingly simple idea that had the potential to significantly streamline the entire operation. They prioritized their ideas according to what they considered to be most vital, and they emphatically agreed that they should move forward. This was a big *Go*. Now they were onto Step Five.

Starting as a Partner or Distributor in a Direct Sales Business

Karen realized that the real issue causing the gap between her current reality and her vision was the lack of a clear plan. She had been attributing her lack of success to being too busy to engage, yet, that wasn't the real issue. That simple "Aha!" moment was eye opening for Karen. Now, it was time to lay the foundation for a plan to help her achieve success.

Her goal was to achieve the gold rank, so I asked her what that meant in numbers. She responded that it was about $10,000 dollars in purchases by her team in a month. I told her that she really needed to know her "close rate" and "average monthly spend" from each team member or customer. For example, if she hosted a party at her house where potential clients could try the product, how many of them would join her team?

We figured out that about one in three at a party would join her team. So, to get three new people on her team, she would need to have at least nine people attend her party. From personal invitations (without a party), her close rate was in the ballpark of one in ten people. We were making progress!

The last question I had for her was the "average monthly spend" for each team member or customer. It came out to be about $175 per month. Now, it was simple math. She had $1,000 coming in each month from her small team that she had built. So, here was the math to get her to gold:

Target income: $10,000/month
Current income: $1,000/month
Difference: $9,000 per month
To make up the difference: With an average monthly spend of $175 per customer, she would need 51 new team members or customers ($9,000 ÷ $175).
To recruit 51 new members: If she was averaging 15 people at a party (that's five new team members per party), she would need to hold at least 11 parties.

With these key numbers in place, we started to brainstorm additional ideas to help her develop a plan to reach gold. Below are a few of her ideas:

1. **Hold one party per month at her house during the next four months.** At a close rate of one in three (and an average number of attendees being 15) this would generate 20 new team members during the next four months. That would still leave a deficit of 31 new customers or team members to reach her goal.

2. **Reach out to at least two people a day via social media or phone.** Her personal close rate wasn't as good as the parties, yet this would still bring in an average of

one new team member or customer per week (her close rate was about one in ten for social media or personal invites). Over the course of four months, that would be an additional 16 team members. With an additional 16 members or customers, she would still have a 14-person deficit from what was required to reach her goal.

3. **Find a women's conference and sponsor the conference.** We identified at least two women's conferences in the upcoming two months where she could be a sponsor for less than $100 and that would give her five minutes during lunch to talk about her booth and product. With several hundred women attending, she only needed to find seven contacts per conference. She about jumped out of her chair when we talked about that idea. With seven people from each conference, she would hit her goal.

4. **Set up a weekly team meeting for her current team members.** The previous three ideas assumed that her current team did nothing, yet she had a great resource in them. They could all be adding team members during this time as well. She wasn't engaging them, so to hold a weekly meeting would help them start developing their respective plans and goals as well. Once she got them up and running, she knew they would do great, but she couldn't expect them to engage without helping them start.

With those four ideas, she was so excited she literally wanted to run out the door and go to work! We were excited, too, but told her to wait until we had completed the entire Six-Step Process. So on to Step Five!

What Does This Step Mean to You?

As you look at your challenges or opportunities, this will be an exciting step for you. Now that you've identified what the real issue is that's keeping you from your vision, you can start developing ideas and decide whether it is a Go or No Go. Remember this old saying, "When you fail to plan, you plan to fail!" Whether you brainstorm or mind-map, this is the time to generate ideas to help you achieve your vision and transform your results going forward. Once you have your finalized list of ideas/solutions, then you can move to Step Five—Develop and Implement the Plan.

YOU DO:

A. WHAT ARE SOME IDEAS, SOLUTIONS, AND OPTIONS THAT WILL HELP YOU ACHIEVE YOUR VISION? YOU CAN EITHER BRAIN-STORM OR MIND-MAP IDEAS.

1.

2.

3.

4.

5.

6.

7.

B. SORT THROUGH THE PREVIOUS LIST AND RANK YOUR IDEAS STARTING WITH THE IDEA THAT WOULD HAVE THE GREATEST IMPACT.

1.

2.

3.

4.

5.

C. ARE THESE IDEAS ETHICAL AND FEASIBLE? ELIMINATE/CROSS OFF THOSE THAT ARE NOT.

D. GO OR NO GO?

CHAPTER 7

Step Five:
Develop and Implement the Plan

This is a great place to hit pause and think about your team. As you consider your team, let's contrast the responses of two different types of employees when they encounter a problem at work. Our first employee will go to their manager with a problem, but no solution or plan to make it better. They tell their supervisor, "We need to produce 25,000 units a month, but we're only producing 16,000 units." End of conversation.

In our experience, this is one of the most common frustrations for managers—employees who bring up a problem, but not a proposed solution to solve the problem. While managers are grateful to be aware of the problem, they now inherit the problem and feel the onerous burden to solve it.

Another unnecessary weight has been added to the shoulders of the manager.

Contrast that example with an employee who is empowered with the Six-Step Process to find solutions and navigate change. They tell their supervisor, "We need 25,000 units a month, but we've only been producing 16,000 units. I went through the Six-Step Process and came up with a plan that I believe will get us there, and I wanted to share it with you to get your thoughts and input."

Wow! As a manager, you would probably feel like shouting hallelujah if an employee said that to you. Imagine the difference between these two types of employees and the impact it would have if you were able to develop employees like you saw in the second example. The Six-Step Process arms employees and managers alike with a process that can be used over and over to navigate change, problem solve, and become solution focused.

Now, let's press play again and get back to where we stand in the Six Steps. Up to this point, the first four steps all laid the foundation for Step Five: Develop and Implement the Plan. In this step, you will take your ideas and solutions and put meat on their bones. In other words, you will figure out *who* will do *what* by *when*. These action steps form the powerful engine that drives the Transformation Challenge. Step Five provides you with the focus, clarity, and plan to achieve your vision and help you become unstoppable.

Your first steps in creating a solid, effective plan are the following:

A. **Invite input from key stakeholders.**
B. **Identify any threats to your ideas and solutions from Step Four.**
C. **Identify any resources you need to implement your ideas from Step Four.**
D. **Review lessons learned from someone who has successfully done what you are doing.**
E. **Identify *Who* will do *What* by *When*.**

F. Evaluate or "red team" the plan. (A red team is an independent party who can provide feedback from an outsider's point of view.)

We'll take a closer look at each of these six actions in a moment. Before doing that, however, we want you to notice that item E is emphasized. Why? Everything about the Six Steps is to get you to the point where you take the solutions you created in Step Four (ideas that address the root cause of the gap between the current reality and vision) and develop a specific plan of *who-what-when*. With that in mind, let's look at each of these actions that will help you create a strong, robust plan.

A. Invite input from key stakeholders

If you are a partner in an organization or an employee putting together a plan that will impact an entire team, you might want to solicit input and ideas from other stakeholders *before* you get to the *who-what-when*. In most cases, you will get additional ideas that you can incorporate into your final plan, and the other key stakeholders will appreciate being included. For example, in an organization, this might be your supervisor, key co-workers, or even a client.

If you are taking the Transformation Challenge for a personal issue, then maybe your key stakeholders would include family members or close friends. Other times, there may not be other stakeholders and you can skip this action item of Step Five.

B. Identify the threats

When talking about a team, threats could be both internal or external. Examine the external environment and identify what the potential threats to the ideas or solutions you generated in Step Four. Examples might include:

- **Oil price increases**
- **Financing**
- **Government regulation**
- **Internet taxation**
- **Labor disputes**
- **Supply chain disruption**
- **Loss of a key team member**
- **Insufficient training**
- **Becoming disabled**

Once you identify the potential threats to your ideas, you can address these threats when you get to the *who-what-when*. When doing a workshop with an organization, we ask the team to identify the top three threats to achieving their Step Four ideas. Then, during the *who-what-when*, they identify specific actions to include in the plan to mitigate those threats.

C. Identify the resources

List the resources you will need to implement your ideas. Examples might include:

- Training: Are the employees adequately trained? What training would be needed to effectively implement this plan? Is there a plan in place to accomplish that training?
- Structure: What is the required infrastructure to accomplish the plan? Is there a physical process in place to handle the logistics flow? If not, what needs to be acquired or set up?
- People: People are typically the greatest resource you have. Has anyone in the organization done this before? Is there a partner or friend who's done this and would be willing to help? Do you have the right people on the bus and in the right seats?
- Technology: What type of technology is required or can be leveraged to help this plan be successful?

- **Financial Resources: Do you have adequate financial resources to accomplish the plan? Exercise extreme caution if the plan is highly leveraged with debt and changes the financial structure of the organization.**

As with the threats, choose the top two or three resources you might need and incorporate any action items into your *who-what-when*.

D. Review lessons learned

The reason fighter pilots are so good at what they do is because they debrief every flight and analyze every aspect of it. Based on the lessons learned from the debrief, they can repeat their successes and eliminate their failures.

How many times in your life and organization have you finished a project and then simply moved onto the next project? For most people and organizations, it happens almost all the time. We strongly suggest that organizations and individuals pause and debrief after a project. Your lessons learned generated during the debrief will help you repeat successes and eliminate failures or future costly mistakes.

During this step, you might review lessons learned that you've accumulated through your experience, or you might hire a consultant or coach who can save you countless hours of time, money, and research. The point is, before the *who-what-when*, you can incorporate any previous lessons learned, either from your experience or someone else's experience, into your plan.

E. Identify *Who* will do *What* by *When*

All roads in the Six-Step Process lead to this action item. Here, you or your team take the ideas and solutions from Step Four—combined with the top threats, required resources, and any lessons learned—and you put it all together in a specific plan that describes *who* will do *what* by *when*.

To see this in action, let's go back to an example from the beginning of the book: a person, Adam, who wants to have better health. In this example, we can see how the entire Six-Step Process comes together to transform a person's results.

Vision (Step #1): To feel full of energy, alive, and healthy!

Current Reality (Step #2): Not exercising; eating poorly; doesn't meditate anymore; is spending 12–13 hours a day in the office; and has a high level of stress.

Identify the Real Issue (Step #3): Adam feels such a high level of pressure to deliver results at work that he hasn't been taking care of himself anymore. Because he doesn't have a plan for himself, he allocates most of his time to work to the point where he feels like he isn't even being an effective leader anymore.

What Are Some Options, Ideas, Solutions (Step #4): Take thirty to sixty minutes each day for his own health; develop a healthy eating plan; start listening to motivating podcasts/audiobooks on the way to and from work; set his vision/goals for the year; hire a health coach to increase accountability; run a half marathon later in the year; and get at least eight hours of sleep each night.

Develop and Implement the Plan (Step #5):
KEY STAKEHOLDERS: Talk with his business partner and spouse about his health and ideas.
THREATS: He couldn't list any major threats. A few minor threats to his ideas are procrastination and lack of accountability.
RESOURCES: A BYB planner, health coach, new running shoes, and a membership to a local gym.

LESSONS LEARNED: He has a friend, Jill, who went through something similar, so he decides to talk with her and get her thoughts.

WHO – WHAT – WHEN: (in this plan, most of the who ends up being him):

WHO	WHAT	WHEN
Adam	Talk with Jill about some of her lessons learned.	By Friday
Adam	Find a health coach and develop a healthy eating plan.	By June 5th
Adam	Invest in a BYB planner, set specific goals for the year, and start pre-week planning to make time for at least an hour a day of reading, meditation, and exercise.	By June 10th
Adam and Business Partner	Visit about the health plan with his business partner to ensure everyone has the same vision and is aligned in helping Adam get his health and energy back.	By June 11th
Adam	Get a membership to the local gym and identify at least one weekly class to attend.	By June 12th
Adam and Spouse	Spend a few minutes together each evening and be in bed by 10:00 p.m. for a solid eight hours of sleep.	By June 12th
Adam	Find a fun half marathon and sign up to run it with at least two friends (accountability).	By July 1st

WHO	WHAT	WHEN
Adam	Run the half marathon.	Before November 25th

That's as far as we'll go in this example. The question is, *Would this plan help Adam transform his health and achieve the vision that he came up with in Step One?* Most would agree that this plan would at least help him transform his *now* while moving significantly closer toward his *vision*.

When you have a plan like the one above, it brings focus and clarity to your life and team. Even the biggest challenges feel like they can be solved when you have an actionable plan.

Here are a few tips to help you with the *who-what-when*:

First, when deciding on *who*, you should almost always use a name or job title. You wouldn't say *marketing department*. There needs to be a single person or title who is ultimately responsible and accountable. If you are doing this for a personal issue, most of the *who* will be you. If doing this with a team, be careful that you don't assign most of the tasks to a single person. You may inadvertently overwhelm them. Of course, there are cases when most action items will fall to one person. It's just something to be aware of.

Second, when writing the *what,* write it so that someone who wasn't there could easily understand it. In workshops, we commonly see team members who initially fail to do this. They might write "Improve communication" or "Fix the customer process." Neither of these likely means anything to someone who wasn't there for the planning meeting. A better way to say the same thing might be, "Develop an inter-department communication plan that high-lights three accomplishments from each department on a weekly basis," or "Conduct a customer walk-through analysis starting with the first inbound call to identify areas of improvement in the customer experience." These examples are so detailed and specific, they're much easier for someone who's not involved in the process to understand the exact parameters of the plan. Try to be specific and detailed in the *what*. The *what* is your action step.

When working with our close friend and the COO of the Dallas Cowboys Merchandising Division, he asked us a great question: "As part of the *what,* can I delegate the Six-Step Process to another team or group?"

The answer is yes! In his case, he used the Six-Step Process to delegate a Six-Step Process to different divisions in the company. By doing so, he transformed a big issue within the organization.

Here's how that would look: "Jim (Marketing Director), you are assigned to use the Six-Step Process to develop a detailed plan to increase website traffic by 15 percent. Lindsay (Warehouse Director), you are assigned to use the Six-Step Process to develop a plan to reduce overhead by 10 percent."

In these examples, a leader delegates to a department head, who then uses the Six-Step Process with their team to develop a plan. The actual *who-what-when* in this delegation example might look like this:

WHO: Jim (Marketing Director)
WHAT: Develop a detailed plan to increase website traffic by 15 percent
WHEN: By July 1st

Jim would now go back with his team and use the Six-Step Process with his team to develop the *who-what-when* to accomplish that objective.

Our final tip is to keep the plan in front of you. If you are individually responsible, post it in your room or next to the computer where you will see it often. If you are doing this with your team, keep it in a place where it's visible and include a follow-up meeting as part of the plan to evaluate results and track progress.

It wouldn't do any good to develop an incredible plan and then stick it in a drawer somewhere.

F. Red Team or Evaluation Team

In the Pentagon, after a team develops a war plan, they invite a group of outsiders to *red team* the plan. In other words, two to four people (typically critical thinkers) are invited to look over the plan and find any holes. It is far better to discover an issue with your plan during the planning phase, rather than the execution phase. A *red team* member might say to the team, "Have you considered that three years ago Jill, from the call center, did something similar to what you had listed and this is what she found?"

What does the *red team* or *evaluation team* mean to you?

If you develop a plan with your team or organization, it would be wise to have a handful of people *red team* your plan before you put it into motion. If taking the Transformation Challenge for a personal issue, maybe a coach, friend, or mentor could help *red team* your plan.

Now, let's go back to our case studies to see how they accomplished Step Five.

A Challenged Marriage

Ben and Lisa had developed a pretty strong list of actionable ideas in Step Four. Now it was time for them to develop the actual plan. Interestingly, after seventeen years of marriage, they had never done anything like this, and they were excited to have a specific way forward.

Here's what they came up with in Step Five:

KEY STAKEHOLDERS: N/A
THREATS: The kids' schedule and being too busy. Pretty simple and straightforward.

RESOURCES REQUIRED: Lisa needs a new BYB planner to do pre-week planning.

LESSONS LEARNED: In this case, they didn't seek out a counselor or anyone else who might be able to help share lessons learned. They marked this N/A.

WHO – WHAT – WHEN:

WHO	WHAT	WHEN
Ben and Lisa	Invest in a BYB planner and individually do pre-week planning every Sunday before 7 p.m. Review our week together before 9 p.m.	Every Sunday evening
Ben and Lisa	Do at least one random act of kindness for the other person during the week.	Weekly
Ben	Schedule a nice dinner to develop joint goals (as a couple) for the rest of the year.	Before March 1st
Ben and Lisa	Identify two weekends for getaways during the year and block them off on the calendar.	Identify dates by March 5th
Lisa	Print off our family standards: no electronics after 8:30 p.m. and spend five minutes together each evening. Post them on the bathroom mirror and next to the computer.	Before March 10th
Ben and Lisa	Go on a date every other week. Rotate who plans the date night—Ben one date and Lisa the next one.	Every other week
Ben and Lisa	Go to dinner to evaluate results and review progress.	July 1st

This was the first time in their marriage that they had ever written a plan like this together—there were a few more action steps to their plan, but you get the idea. Both Ben and Lisa were excited and a little nervous to see if they would follow through and accomplish it. Now that they had a physical plan they could refer to, they could already sense the transformation that was taking place in their relationship. They felt aligned in a way that they hadn't felt in years.

Lisa printed a copy of the Who – What – When and put it next to their bed and in the office. She didn't want all that emotion and energy to just get tossed away in a drawer somewhere.

What happened? How well did Ben and Lisa follow their new plan? You'll find out in the next chapter.

Flying J

Flying J was at a critical point. They had enough viable ideas to save the company; now they needed a specific plan to execute those ideas. Here is what they came up with:

> **KEY STAKEHOLDERS:** The Board of Directors, creditors, attorneys, banks, and the employees. The team solicited input from each of these groups to ensure that they had the necessary information to build a solid plan and maintain a high level of communication.
>
> **THREATS:** Since the banks had called the loans, there was a real threat of asset seizure such as bank accounts, pipeline, and accounts receivable. There was also a threat of real estate seizure because of its association with the travel centers, which would force store closures. The loss of key employees because of job security concerns.
>
> **RESOURCES:** Access to cash for continuing operations. Protection from banks and creditors to prevent asset seizure. Time to reorganize and work through the problems and issues that created the cash crisis.

LESSONS LEARNED: They hired a law firm with a lot of experience in bankruptcy and helping other organizations that had unexpected setbacks and challenges.

WHO – WHAT – WHEN:

WHO	WHAT	WHEN
Crystal	Meet with the executive committee and bankruptcy attorneys to develop a plan to save the company.	December 1, 2008
Kirkland & Ellis and Young Conaway Stargatt & Taylor LLP.	File for Chapter 11 Bankruptcy to have protection from banks and creditors to reorganize the company.	December 22, 2008
Crystal	Effect the change of president to Crystal because of philosophical differences on how to lead the company and which direction it should take.	January 5, 2009
Crystal	Communicate with all employees the plan to "Save the Company." Put out a regular communication bulletin with updates and progress on the reorganizing plan.	January 10, 2009 with monthly communication
Crystal and the reorganizing committee	Sell the oil refinery in Bakersfield, CA.	September 1, 2009
Crystal and the reorganizing committee	Sell the 700-mile Gulf pipeline.	September 1, 2009

WHO	WHAT	WHEN
Crystal and the reorganizing committee	Find a partner, through merger or sale, of the Flying J Travel Centers.	September 1, 2009
Crystal and the reorganizing committee	Work legal representatives and courts to emerge from Bankruptcy having satisfied all creditors and banks.	January 2011
Crystal and the reorganizing committee	Have a new company that is healthy, viable, and well structured as a partner in the travel center business and/ or gas station-convenience store markets.	January 2011

Because of this plan, there was a new hope and energy that spread throughout the organization. What originally seemed impossible to most employees and advisers was now well within reach. There was light at the end of this ominously dark tunnel.

Everyone understood the vision and the plan. Each person in the company knew they played a role in its success, and they went to work.

Was it a success? Were they able to save the company and fulfill their plan? You'll find out in the next chapter what happened to Flying J and where they are today.

Shawn and the Eighteen Months of Unemployment

As Shawn and I finished the final yards of the 5K, he was excited about the ideas we had brainstormed in Step Four. What he still lacked was the specific plan of *who – what – when*. His next job interview was only a few days away, so time was of the essence. Even though the 5K was over, we decided to finish Step Five together before leaving.

KEY STAKEHOLDERS: Shawn visited with his wife and shared the ideas with her. She was surprised, excited, and very supportive.

THREATS: Financial pressures, health, emotional state of mind, and Shawn's confidence.

RESOURCES: Shawn's talents and experience, Steve and Shawn's family and friends.

LESSONS LEARNED: I had coached numerous people and knew that with practice and role-playing, Shawn could regain his confidence. The other lesson learned that I shared with Shawn is to focus on the vision of his employer in the interview and to talk about them and their success rather than talking about himself.

WHO – WHAT – WHEN (remember to include a date to evaluate progress):

WHO	WHAT	WHEN
Shawn	Write the Six-Step plan and put it in a place where he would see it daily.	May 15th
Shawn	Revise the résumé. Instead of putting NA in the Bachelor's Degree, replace it with the Bachelors of Life.	May 15th
Shawn	Shave his beard and dress professionally for the interview.	May 15th
Shawn and Steve	Meet with Steve to review my résumé, identify interview questions, practice, and role-play the job interview.	May 16th

WHO	WHAT	WHEN
Shawn	Go to job interview and have fun. Share my vision and keep the interview focused on how to help the owners sleep well at night.	May 18th
Shawn	If offered the job, develop a plan to ensure maximum productivity and contribution.	May 20th
Shawn and Steve	Meet to evaluate results and develop lessons learned, if necessary.	May 24th

Considering that Shawn had been unemployed for eighteen months, this plan was a big step for him. As mentioned previously, he was highly qualified, but had lost his confidence.

Just as we've seen many times when people and organizations use the Six-Step Process, Shawn felt a surge of optimism and excitement because his path forward was clear. He only had a few days to implement the plan, so he went home that afternoon and got started.

Would the plan work for Shawn, despite his short amount of time before the interview? Would he get the job, or remain unemployed? We'll find out in Step Six.

A Business with a Broken Process and Millions of Dollars on the Line

The team at Eagle involved in the planning process was excited about their ideas from Step Four. They gathered around the table to take those ideas and put together the plan.

KEY STAKEHOLDERS: The program manager at the utility, as well as the managers at Eagle (those involved with this program).

THREATS: Eagle could be dropped as a contractor for this program due to non-compliance. If eliminated, this could affect all the contracts that Eagle had with the utility in their other divisions. If this issue wasn't fixed, it would significantly tarnish the reputation of Eagle as being a "best in class" company.

RESOURCES: New software to run the proposed reporting program as well as tablets for each technician.

LESSONS LEARNED: In this case, the people with the experience and lessons learned were in the room. The big lesson learned was that the relationship with the utility was the most important thing, and they needed to communicate exactly what was happening so that everyone was in the loop and expectations were managed well.

WHO – WHAT – WHEN:

WHO	WHAT	WHEN
Matt	Share the Six Steps with the other employees and stakeholders within Eagle to make sure there was total buy-in.	June 25th
Matt and Doug	Present and propose Six-Steps outline as a "white paper" to the utility to get their feedback and buy-in.	July 8th
Charles Wright and Adam Edwards	Get feedback and next steps from utility leadership on the proposed plan.	August 1st
Matt and Doug	If the plan is approved, purchase the tablets.	August 10th

WHO	WHAT	WHEN
Alejandro	Complete all software support systems to implement the new process on tablets.	August 15th
Matt and Doug	Hold technician, outreach, and administrative training on the new process and system.	August 18th
Matt and Doug	Test the new process and system in a pilot program with a couple of technicians.	August 20th
Matt and Doug	Implement and put into action the new process and plan. Have a kick-off meeting.	September 1st
Donna and Lori	Track the results daily, debrief, and ensure daily compliance reports are shared with key stakeholders.	September 1st and report weekly to Eagle and utility
Matt, Doug and All Key Stakeholders	Evaluate the success and any shortcomings in the new process and system. Develop lessons learned and implement any changes.	October 1st

Matt and the entire team were thrilled with the plan. Assuming the utility approved the plan, the Eagle team knew they could execute it and that it would get them back in compliance.

What seemed like a daunting and impossible task just a few days prior was now clearly achievable and it brought a new spirit of excitement and optimism to the team.

In the next chapter, you'll see what happened to Eagle, not only in the ensuing months, but also in subsequent years.

Starting as a Partner or Distributor in a Direct Sales Business

We had just finished a great brainstorm with Karen in Step Four, and together we developed some ideas that would launch her toward her vision and goal. She was thrilled and couldn't wait to get to work, but we had to remind her that the actual plan needed to be finished.

Here's what we came up with together in Step Five:

KEY STAKEHOLDERS: N/A

THREATS: She was concerned about her follow through and accountability.

RESOURCES: She would need a list of women's conferences with two hundred or less attendees and she needed to add more friends to her social media accounts. Since she was unfamiliar with social media marketing campaigns, we decided to have her hire a third-party service to use targeted ads.

LESSONS LEARNED: She had a close friend who was very successful in that company, so part of the plan would include a lunch with this friend to find out what lessons she had learned.

WHO – WHAT – WHEN:

WHO	WHAT	WHEN
Karen	Reach out to at least two friends or associates every day, either via text, email, or phone.	Daily
Karen	Set up a lunch with her successful friend to get additional lessons learned and ideas.	By December 3rd

WHO	WHAT	WHEN
Rob	Send Karen a list of third-party social media marketing companies.	By December 5th
Karen	Schedule four home parties during the next four months—one per month. Get the dates on the calendar and invites sent through text, email, and direct mail. Target number is a minimum of fifteen attendees.	By December 8th
Karen	Develop a list of all current and past friends or associates. Send them invites to connect on Instagram, Facebook, and LinkedIn.	By December 11th
Karen	Find a list of women's associations and conferences with less than two hundred attendees. Once Karen has the list, send it to Rob for his review and select the two best candidates to sponsor before March.	By December 15th
Karen	Choose a weekly time and day to set up a training meeting rhythm for current team members (in anticipation of growing the team).	By December 15th
Karen and Rob	Phone meeting with Rob to evaluate progress and make any plan adjustments.	January 10th

Over the course of less than two hours, Karen had gone from a place of frustration and fading hope to a place of growing excitement and action. Like the other stories, she felt like she had a clear path forward. She was leading a life by design rather than a life by default. With a plan, she felt empowered and in control of her fate.

My comment to her was that some things will go as planned and others won't. That is why we set up the meeting on January 10th to evaluate her progress, develop lessons learned, and adjust as necessary. I also reminded her that a person is 90 percent more likely to accomplish something when they have a clearly written goal and plan. She had just tipped the scales strongly in her favor! Where would her plan lead her? Would her excitement and enthusiasm last? We'll find out in the final step.

What Does This Step Mean to You?

Think about how different you are now from the masses. Most people go right from problem to execution and then wonder why nothing has changed. After the first Four Steps, it is time for you to develop and implement *your* plan. Remember, the plan is *who – what – when!* The whole point of the Six-Step Process is to develop your action plan. When you finish developing your plan, the litmus test is this question: *If you follow that plan (who – what – when), will you address the root cause that is causing the gap between your current reality and your vision?* If so, get excited and go to work!

YOU DO:

This is your chance to practice Step Five—Develop and Implement the Plan. You will take the ideas and solutions from Step Four and develop the action plan (who – what – when) to achieve your vision.

KEY STAKEHOLDERS:

_____

_____

_____

THREATS (internal or external):

_____

_____

_____

RESOURCES (what resources might you need):

_____

_____

_____

LESSONS LEARNED (who has done this successfully):

_____

_____

_____

WHO – WHAT – WHEN (remember to include a date to evaluate progress):

WHO	WHAT	WHEN

CHAPTER 8

Step Six:
Debrief and Evaluate Results

The entire purpose of the Six-Step Process is to improve. It offers a reliable, powerful way to engineer better results, solve problems, and develop opportunities. It helps you address the most important issues in your life—those that affect your happiness, peace, productivity, and the success of your organizations. And it empowers you to lead your life, family, and team. These steps arm you with a repeatable process—a standard operating procedure—to navigate change and transform your results.

In your organization, you can fuse the Six-Step Process into your culture. Remember, you will either have a culture by design or you will have a culture by default. It is much easier to establish a culture when founded on solid processes so that people aren't left to guess what is right.

By this point, if you've navigated the first five steps of the process, you've come a long way from your starting point. Now, in Step Six, you get a chance to step back, debrief, and evaluate your results. The debrief is all about the pivot and course correction. You identify what is working well and what's not working and then develop lessons learned to repeat the successes and eliminate the failures.

Step Six doesn't just happen after your *Who – What – When*. You should build in debrief and evaluation dates into the *Who – What – When* plan, as well as have a debrief after the plan is complete.

In other words, during the execution of your plan, you should pause to assess your progress and ask whether you are on track. If you are, great. If not, what adjustments need to be made to course correct?

After you have finished executing your plan (*Who – What – When*), you pause again to debrief your results. Did you get the results you wanted and did you accomplish the vision? If so, great—time to apply the Six-Step Process to another issue. If not, what are the lessons learned so that you can repeat the successes and eliminate any failures as you go back to Step One and reassess the vision? This is the reason that the illustration of the Six-Step Process shows it flowing in a continuous circle.

Remember, the *debrief* is what makes fighter pilots so good at what they do. After every flight, every sortie, the pilots will take between one to eight hours to debrief. The debrief is nameless and rankless, which removes ego and keeps everyone focused on *what's* right, not *who's* right.

The debrief has one primary objective: identify the root cause for the successes and failures so that successes can be repeated in future flights and failures can be minimized or eliminated. Step Six is the debrief zone.

Look at this step as if you were a fighter pilot. As we already mentioned, it is important for you to include debrief or evaluation dates in the *Who – What – When* plan. These are built-in pause buttons where you assess your progress. For example, it might say in the middle of the plan:

WHO: Jim
WHAT: Marketing Team Midcourse debrief to assess progress
WHEN: April 1st

This practice of debriefing inoculates us against the tendency to blitz from project to project in a mad dash. When most people or teams finish a project or plan, they high-five each other, or pat themselves on the back, and move on to the next project. They never pause to identify lessons that can be applied in the future.

While it may seem counterintuitive to slow down, it's a huge boost for your productivity. Why? While your body may be taking a break from tasks, your brain shifts into high analytical gear to evaluate—and learn from—what just happened.

Remember in Step Five, just before you created the *Who – What – When*, you were invited to review lessons learned. Those lessons learned typically come from two places—other people who have experienced a similar challenge or lessons you learn from a debrief.

With that in mind, here are your debriefing questions:

1. **Were your vision and goals clearly articulated?**
2. **Did you fully capture the current reality, both positive or challenging aspects of the issue?**
3. **Did you ask why, why, why and get to the *real* root cause of the issue causing the gap between the current reality and the vision?**
4. **Did you create an environment within your team where the best ideas could come forward to provide the basis for a strong plan of action to solve the problem or develop the opportunity?**
5. **Did you set up a plan of action based on the best ideas, including *who* would do *what* by *when?* Was the plan**

communicated to all key stakeholders to maximize your chance for success? Did you have a *red team* review the plan and offer suggestions? What worked well and what didn't work so well? Why?
6. **Did you pause to debrief and evaluate results during the execution of the plan? What lessons learned did you identify? How could you have improved?**

This powerful step is often one of the most overlooked, yet it can be one of the most important. This is particularly true when dealing with complex or ongoing issues such as a manufacturing issue, a sales issue, improving a relationship, or having better health.

Let's check in with the people in our case studies and see how they fared in executing their plans and how Step Six helped them.

A Challenged Marriage

Ben and Lisa finished Step Five excited and filled with hope. They decided to schedule a dinner as part of their plan to evaluate how they were doing along the way. It was late February when they developed the plan and they decided to schedule a dinner for July 1st to evaluate their results.

July arrived. They went to their scheduled dinner, and started the debrief by reviewing some of their successes.

- They both invested in a BYB planner and had been consistent in their pre-week planning. They each missed one or two weeks along the way, but by and large they did well. Simply doing pre-week planning and then reviewing their week together each Sunday had a huge impact on their marriage. They credited this action as one of the things that truly transformed their relationship and brought them back together again. They revised the phrase, *a culture by design* and coined the term, "Creating a marriage by design rather than a marriage by default." This action item in their plan had helped them be very focused and intentional about their time and marriage, week in and week out.

- As planned, they went to dinner and developed some joint goals together. This was exciting for them because it was the first time in their marriage that they had joint goals and they were on track to do several things they had never done together.

- In late spring, they found a babysitter for the kids and spent a weekend at a nearby mountain resort. It was a wonderful weekend together and they couldn't wait until the Fall when they would do it again.

- After reviewing their successes, they defined areas that needed improvement:

- One of the "What" items was to "Print off our *family standards* of no electronics after 8:30 p.m. and spend five minutes together each evening. Post them on the bathroom mirror and next to the computer." This part of their plan slipped through the cracks and never got done. They both laughed as they realized that their nightly ritual was for each of them to spend about ten minutes looking at their phones while lying in bed. Lisa told Ben that she would write the "standards" and print them the next day. They both recommitted to no electronics after 8:30 p.m.

- Although they had been on many more dates together than they ever had prior to the Transformation Challenge, they still missed a handful of weeks. They asked *why* and realized that it simply hadn't been a part of the discussion during their weekly planning on Sunday. They made that adjustment and committed to making that a part of their discussion so that they stay on track.

What was the result of Ben and Lisa taking the Transformation Challenge and using the Six-Step Process? It literally transformed their marriage and relationship.

Naturally, that's great for them, but they weren't the only ones transformed. Think about the ripple effect on future generations of this family—starting with their own children. A happy marriage with parents who genuinely love each other can have a powerful effect on the lasting happiness and success of children.

Prior to the Transformation Challenge Ben and Lisa felt like they had a *good* relationship, but there was no doubt they were beginning to drift apart and they both felt the strain on their marriage.

Was their marriage perfect after the Transformation Challenge? No. However, it was a huge step in the right direction. As a result, they invested time and energy in each other, they rekindled fire and passion in their relationship, and they were—day by day and week by week—creating a marriage by design rather than by default. They were excited for their future together and in just a few months they had experienced a dramatic shift in their marriage and relationship!

Flying J

Crystal and her team immediately went to work on the action items as part of their plan to *save the company*. They debriefed several times during the execution of the plan and made necessary adjustments to the plan to stay on track. What was the ultimate result?

Flying J came out of chapter 11 bankruptcy eighteen months later after satisfying 100 percent of their obligations. After emerging from Chapter 11, they were poised to be a dominant force in the industry.

They ended up selling and merging their Flying J Travel Centers with Pilot Travel Centers, while retaining their other operations under the new FJ Management Company. This merger, with an incredible partner, allowed the new group of travel centers to be the predominant travel center company throughout the United States.

The refinery and pipeline were sold, providing much needed capital, while allowing Crystal and her team to focus on the business units that had the greatest profit potential.

The company was saved and FJ Management was well positioned to be one of the premier companies in their industry, which was a part of Crystal's new vision. Crystal and her team had accomplished the seemingly impossible of saving company. They achieved a stronger position than ever before.

At the time of this writing, it has been six years since the company was saved and reorganized. FJ Management has successfully branched into other verticals and is thriving. They have launched a new line of convenience stores named *Maverick* and they are dominating in almost every geographic region where they are located.

Shawn and the Eighteen Months of Unemployment

Shawn fully implemented his plan of *Who – What – When*.

He revised his résumé. He shaved and looked sharp. He went to Steve's house on Saturday and role played the interview that he would have on Monday. The primary focus of the role play was Shawn's vision and the difference that he could make in the organization he was interviewing with. He visualized and practiced the tough questions he knew would come—questions about his background, his experience, and the last eighteen months.

Together, we practiced his answers over and over, not until he got them right, but until he couldn't get them wrong. Shawn was ready for the interview on Monday, emotionally, physically, and mentally. He was excited!

The interview on Monday was scheduled with a premier software company. It went amazingly well, just as planned. They asked about his Bachelor's of Life and Shawn explained that because of his experience in the marketing world, he had indeed obtained far more than a diploma, he had a Bachelor's of Life because of his experience. This certainly piqued the interest of the interviewers and everyone was engaged and wanted to know more about Shawn. This question about his Bachelor's used to be an obstacle, now he turned it into an opportunity.

The interviewers then asked Shawn what his vision was and how he felt like he could contribute. Thanks to our role playing, that question was right in his wheelhouse! He had practiced answering it numerous times. Prepared, confident, and calm, he shared his short vision and then added that part of his vision was to help them sleep well at night. They loved it!

They invited Shawn back on Tuesday for a follow-up interview. During the interview, they had additional people in the room as well as the executives who were there from the first interview. The executives from the first interview asked Shawn to repeat the part about helping the owners sleep well at night and how he would do that. Again, he was ready and everyone in the room loved his answers that he had practiced over and over.

Shawn was invited back, for yet a third interview with the key decision makers where a job offer was made. The salary they offered was significantly higher than Shawn expected and it included full benefits. Shawn accepted, and the long, draining eighteen months of unemployment were over. He became fully engaged in the work force.

At the time of this writing, it has been three years since Shawn started working with the firm that hired him. He has certainly helped the owners sleep well at night, which has resulted in several awards. He has been promoted several times and is now considered to be one of the key managers and employees in the organization!

By taking the Transformation Challenge during a 5K walk, Shawn took a situation where he felt hopeless and within a few days landed a high-paying job. Because of this experience and his transformation, he and his family have never been happier!

A Business with a Broken Process and Millions of Dollars on the Line

Matt reviewed the action plan that was intended to bring life back into the relationship with the utility and get their team in compliance.

After the plan was finalized internally, Matt enlisted the utility as his red team to review their plan, the Six Steps, and share any insights. The utility was so impressed with the plan and the entire Six-Step Process that they asked if they could adopt the same process within their own organization. Plus, they were excited and optimistic about Eagle's plan, and they were hyped to see it in action.

As Matt implemented the plan (*Who – What – When*), they would pause about every two weeks to debrief and ensure they were on track. As you might expect, they made small adjustments, but they closely followed the plan, which yielded phenomenal results.

The plan shaved about six days off the paperwork turn-around, taking it from nine days to less than three—well within the compliance-mandated five-day turnaround.

In addition, because of the new system, Eagle saved $25,000 per year in administrative costs, as did the utility. These were huge wins for both parties. The utility applauded Matt and his team because they transformed this volatile, deteriorating situation into an incredibly profitable, rewarding one. They had streamlined a once-broken process that now saved everyone a lot of time, energy, and money.

This happened several years ago. Since then, two major developments have occurred.

First, because of this complete turnaround in service and the tremendous positive relationship it created, Eagle's contract for this program was expanded by $1 million per year.

Two years later, the manager of that service program at the utility was transferred to run the Small Business and Commercial group. Because of the transformational experience he had with

Eagle, he suggested that Eagle apply to provide service in the small business and commercial segment—a segment Eagle had not been in. As a result, over the next couple of years (and to present), Eagle has completed over $30 million worth of work in this segment.

Because of the Transformation Challenge and the Six-Step Process, Eagle solved their issue with compliance and put themselves in position to expand revenue by many millions more than they were making from that single program.

What would have happened if Eagle had not used the Six-Step Process? It's important to consider this alternate reality; without the Six-Step Process, Eagle would have been left to "wing it." As we pointed out earlier in the book, winging it is precisely what happens in many organizations who do not have a codified process in place to approach issues.

But, they didn't wing it. Matt said it was amazing to have a team that all understood the same process and spoke the same problem-solving language. They experienced very little confrontation or contention during the process. They faced an issue that seemed impossible to solve and transformed it into a significant profit for the company.

This was not a one-time event. Today, Eagle consistently uses the Six-Step Process throughout their organization. They have woven it into their culture, and it has resulted in millions in revenue, as well as a much happier and positive work environment!

Starting as a Partner or Distributor in a Direct Sales Business

It was early December when Karen developed her plan. We set up a one-month debrief call in January to evaluate her progress and make any adjustments to her plan. I'll never forget when she walked out of the office with her plan in hand. She exclaimed, "I've never felt so excited and clear about the way forward!"

It didn't take long for Karen to start knocking it out of the park. She stuck to the plan and held several meetings at her home with the predicted results. She also attended a women's conference and generated numerous leads that helped propel her toward her goal.

She implemented her plan to nurture additional team members as they came on board so that they would start building their own teams, too. The more success her team experienced, the more success she experienced.

Did everything go exactly as planned? Of course not. There were a couple of areas where she let up and didn't follow through. Which is why this step, Step Six, is so important. It gives you a chance to pause, evaluate progress, and course correct.

At the time of this writing, Karen is on track to achieve her vision and goal. Before taking the Transformation Challenge and applying the Six-Step Process, she didn't have a plan, was discouraged, and had lost hope. She took what initially seemed like an impossible target and suddenly it became very possible. Over the course of just a few months, she achieved results she had once only dreamed of.

Achieving her goal, however, is not the end. Once attained, it's time to apply the Six-Step Process again to set a new vision and work toward transforming it into reality.

What Does This Step Mean to You?

How often do you pause to debrief and evaluate results and then make the necessary adjustments? From this point forward, the hope is that this step will become a significant part of your personal life and the culture within your organization. Always remember, you will have a culture by design or a culture by default. The debrief and evaluation step can be an exciting one for your team because it gives everyone a voice to make the team better and improve your results.

YOU DO:

1. In your Who – What – When, include dates to debrief and evaluate your results and progress.

2. As part of this step, put your plan in a place where you and/ or your team can evaluate the progress on a daily or weekly basis. In other words, don't develop a great plan and then stick it in a drawer. Where can you put your plan so that you can reference it often?

3. When will you evaluate the entire plan to see whether you have accomplished your vision or whether you need to go through the Six Steps again (choose a date)?

4. After your evaluation and debrief, what are some of your lessons learned so that you can repeat successes and eliminate failures in your future plans?

Conclusion

This book is about your success—and not just a temporary or short-term success. The Six-Step Process will help you successfully navigate change and transform any problem or opportunity that arises in your life or with your team.

In the beginning of the book we mentioned that in our research, not a single company out of 50 had a common approach or process to problem solve or navigate change. Every manager, in fact, had their own technique and style. When it came to problem solving, it was as if team members tried to communicate with each other in a foreign language. Not surprisingly, this random approach to problem-solving sparked frustration and a lot of missed opportunities. In many cases, this miscommunication and lack of planning resulted in millions of dollars in lost revenue and countless hours of wasted energy.

As you've seen throughout this book, it doesn't have to be that way any longer. When people and organizations take the Transformation Challenge and use the Six-Step Process, it aligns the team, invites collaboration, and helps them solve even the most complex issues in a positive way. The result is that it will often save you time, energy, and a lot of money.

You've heard us mention it several times throughout this book, *you will either lead a life by design or you will live a life by default!* When you have a solid plan, you put yourself and your team in a position to win.

As you get ready to turn the last page of this book, you may be asking, what now? To get the greatest results in your life and with your team, here are two ideas that will help you be a catalyst for others and accelerate your results faster:

1. If you haven't already done it, take a real issue in your life or your organization and take the Transformation Challenge—apply the Six-Step Process to that issue. Don't procrastinate and wait until later. There's an adage that says, "The art is in the start. You don't have to be great to start, but you have to start to be great!" This is your invitation to start.

If you would like a free Six-Step Process Quick Start Guide, visit www.TheTransformationChallenge.com and enter your name and email. We'll send you a free Quick Start Guide that you can use over and over.

2. Invite someone else to take the Transformation Challenge. Almost everyone you know either has a problem or challenge that they are struggling with. Oftentimes we may not realize the extent of a problem in a friend or family members life. No matter how big or small the issue, you can be the catalyst to help those you know get to a better place. We invite you to invest in a copy of this book for friends, family, or co-workers and give it to them as a gift. Many times, a leader or manager will get a copy of the book for their entire team. They will have them read it, choose a real issue that applies to their job, and apply the Six-Step Process to come up with a plan to improve that area. This is a way that you can be a force for good in the world. You never know when you will be the person that helps someone else make a life-changing pivot. You can be the spark.

We invite you to briefly pause and make a list of five people who you could send this book to now. As you write their names, think about why this book would be helpful to them:

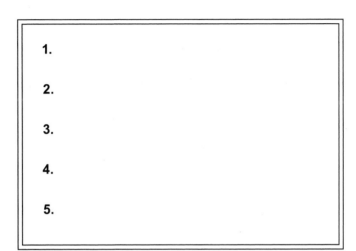

This is the beginning of a journey. It's about bringing hope and excitement into your life and team. The Six-Step Process can transform almost any issue and illuminate a clear way forward, even when it may seem difficult or even impossible.

You are going to have some amazing experiences as you take The Transformation Challenge and continue to apply the Six-Step Process. The natural human tendency is to discount your story and think that nobody would like to hear about it—that's not true! Your story may be the spark to ignite a fire in another person. Most people finish a project and move on. Simply by reading this book, you are not "most people." That's why we invite you to share your story. The process is simple, once you've taken the Transformation Challenge, please share your successes and/or stories with us at support@BecomingYourBest.com.

We wish you the greatest success, both personally, in your families, and in your organizations as you take the Transformation Challenge!

ACCELERATE RESULTS IN YOUR ORGANIZATION!

AWARD-WINNING TRAINING TO HELP YOUR TEAM ACHIEVE THEIR FULLEST POTENTIAL.

KEYNOTES: BYB keynotes will help you deliver an experience that is fun, engaging, and empowering. A BYB keynote is customized to your group and will be an experience that your members or employees will talk about for years to come.

WORKSHOPS AND SEMINARS: Whether in a half-day or multi-day format, a BYB seminar is a customized experience that helps your managers and employees learn cutting edge tools and processes to get long-term results. These seminars are hands-on and address real-world issues that your organization is facing right now.

TRAINER CERTIFICATION: Get certified as a Becoming Your Best trainer and take this content wide and deep throughout your entire organization.

EXECUTIVE COACHING: One on one executive coaching can help leaders navigate change and solve complex issues with simple, proven techniques and a wealth of executive experience.

To schedule a keynote or to discuss how to customize an experience for your group call 1-888-690-8764 or visit www.BecomingYourBest.com

Tools and Resources

The BYB Store provides you with useful tools to use personally or share with your team. From planners to posters, visit the BYB Store today and see what tools can help you.

MOTIVATIONAL POSTERS

BYB PLANNERS   MP3S

Visit the BYB Store Today
www.Store.BecomingYourBest.com

Motivational Posters, Books, Planners, MP3s, and More.

About the Authors

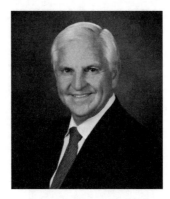

STEVEN SHALLENBEGRER

Steve has more than forty years of experience as a successful business owner, trusted senior executive, professional corporate trainer, and #1 national best-selling author.

After graduating from Brigham Young University in 1976, Steve launched a global leadership and management consulting firm. He has successfully led companies in four different industries and has a keen understanding of how to thrive in business. During those formative years, he continued his education at the Harvard Business School. Steve also worked many years with Stephen R. Covey. As a key leader, among others, he helped build the world-renowned Covey Leadership Center. He's taken his lifetime of experience and founded Becoming Your Best Global Leadership LLC, a company devoted to helping individuals and organizations achieve their maximum potential!

Steve served as president of the Brigham Young University Alumni Association. He was a former president of America's Freedom Foundation and he currently sits on their board of trustees. He was a charter member and chair of the Utah chapter of the Young Presidents' Organization (YPO).

Steve is passionate about his family, having fun, and helping others achieve their potential in life.

ROBERT SHALLENBERGER

Rob is one of the leading global authorities on leadership and strategic planning. He is a highly sought-after keynote speaker, corporate trainer, executive coach and best-selling author. He's trained hundreds of organizations around the world.

After spending two years of service in Bolivia, he attended Utah State University, where he graduated in 2000 with a degree in Marketing. He went on to earn an MBA from Colorado State University. He then served as an F-16 Fighter Pilot in the Air Force for eleven years. He was also an Advance Agent for Air Force One and traveled the world working with foreign embassies and the Secret Service.

He's the CEO of Becoming Your Best Global Leadership. His company released a national best-selling book titled *Becoming Your Best: The 12 Principles of Highly Successful Leaders*. He's also the author of the book *How to Succeed in High School*.

Rob considers his greatest accomplishment to be that he's been married for nineteen years and has four beautiful children.